QUAKER JOURNALS

HOWARD HAINES BRINTON (1884-
1973) made many contributions to the
Society of Friends, but none was more
valuable than his definition of its faith and
practice. As Director Emeritus living on
the Pendle Hill campus he devoted his last
years to works on Quakerism, among
them *Quaker Journals,* first published in
1972 and here reprinted with the author's
original preface.

Other Paperbacks by
HOWARD H. BRINTON
FRIENDS FOR 300 YEARS
GUIDE TO QUAKER PRACTICE

QUAKER JOURNALS

*Varieties of Religious Experience
Among Friends*

HOWARD H. BRINTON

PENDLE HILL PUBLICATIONS

Wallingford, Pennsylvania

QUAKER JOURNALS

Copyright © 1972 by Pendle Hill

For information address Pendle Hill
Wallingford, Pennsylvania   19086

*This reprint has been sponsored
by*
The Miles White Fund of Baltimore Yearly Meeting
and
The Monthly Meeting of Friends of Philadelphia

ISBN 0-87574-908-9
Library of Congress catalog card number: 78-188399
Paperback edition 2,000, June 1983

*Printed in the United States of America by
Lithographic Publications Inc.*

CONTENTS

Preface

DURING the past four years, my course at Pendle Hill on Quakerism has included the study of the Quaker Journals, or spiritual autobiographies. It is necessary to use the qualifying word, "spiritual," because these autobiographies contain very little material about the writers' families and undertakings not directly related to their inner life.

I do not know how many Quaker Journals there are, including those not in print. My guess is that there are probably about a thousand altogether. In this book I am confining my quotations to the three hundred Journals in my own library, hoping that these are fair representatives of Quaker Journals in general.

Since I am too blind to read, I have depended on helpers. For typing the manuscript and locating quotations, I owe much to Marion Glaeser. I am especially indebted to my daughter, Lydia Brinton Forbes, for similar help and for editing the material. I have received indispensable aid from my granddaughter, Joanna Brinton, and from Yuki Takahashi, who was formerly my secretary in Japan. I am also much indebted to the members of the Publications Committee of the Pendle Hill Board, who have read the manuscript, and especially to its secretary, editor of Pendle Hill Publications, Eleanore Price Mather.

I am grateful to the Anna H. and Elizabeth M. Chace Fund for underwriting the cost of this book. Since I was personally acquainted with Elizabeth Chace and have discussed religious problems with her, I am confident that the type of Quakerism portrayed in the Journals during the first century and a half of Quaker history and later represented by the Wilburite group to which she belonged, is the kind with which she would agree. In my opinion, this type is the closest to that of the three important founders of Quakerism: George Fox, William Penn, and Robert Barclay.

Introduction

BECAUSE Quakerism is primarily a religion based on inner personal experience rather than on creed or ritual, the religious autobiography, usually called a "Journal," has been the most characteristic form of Quaker writing.

I know of two books in which Quaker Journals are described by devoting one chapter to each Journalist included in that study. One of these was written by John Greenleaf Whittier. It is entitled *Old Portraits and Modern Sketches* (Boston: Ticknor, Reed, and Fields, 1850). Whittier deals with three Quakers, Thomas Ellwood, James Nayler, John Roberts, and also with a number of other writers, mostly Puritans. In 1968 Daniel B. Shea, Jr. wrote a book entitled *Spiritual Autobiography in Early America* (Princeton University Press) which also deals with Quakers and Puritans. In this he devotes a chapter to each of five Quakers: John Churchman, Thomas Chalkley, David Ferris, Elizabeth Ashbridge, and John Woolman.

There is a certain advantage in devoting a whole chapter to one Journalist as, by that method, we can get a much clearer picture of the individual concerned. In this book, however, I shall deal with the Journalists collectively, principally with those writing in the 17th and 18th centuries. This enables me to deal with many more Journals than would be possible if I endeavored to describe each one individually. And by this method we can get a clearer picture of the way in which Quaker Journals follow very much the same pattern in spite of important individual differences.

The Varieties of Religious Experience (New York: Longmans, Green, 1902) by William James marked an important new epoch in the study of religion. James was an empiricist and, accordingly, devoted his book to religious *experience* rather than to descriptions of theology, ritual, and church organization. I shall follow James's example in pointing out the various stages of spiritual progress which each Journalist believed that he passed through. Most of James's categories of experience can be found in the Quaker Journals.

The only Quaker Journal quoted by James is that of George Fox. It is quoted in order to show how eccentric and absurd a great religious leader can be. Fortunately he prefaces his account by saying:

> The Quaker religion which he founded is something which it is impossible to overpraise. In a day of shams, it was a religion of veracity rooted in spiritual inwardness, and a return to something more like the original gospel truth than men had ever known in England. So far as our Christian sects to-day are evolving into liberality, they are simply reverting in essence to the position which Fox and the early Quakers so long ago assumed. (1904 ed., p. 7).

Many modern Quakers do not know how liberal their founder really was.

James can describe the various stages of spiritual progress in the autobiographies which he quotes because he confines himself largely to the experience of conversion. He includes many other types of religious experience, but his attention is centered on that one. I am confining my attention to one variety of autobiography: Journals written by Quakers.

One difficulty with James's book is that it deals mostly with the experience of geniuses such as St. Augustine or Tolstoy. (Some one has called James's book, "Wild Religions I Have Met.")

I shall deal with the experiences of ordinary persons: farmers, housewives, merchants, shoemakers, doctors, and others, educated or less educated, but with one peculiar quality. They were nearly all traveling ministers of the Society of Friends. They were not in any sense professional ministers. Far from it. They supported themselves by some simple calling—if it had not been simple they would not have had time to travel in the ministry. Many radically limited their businesses in order to devote time to travel. This was not difficult because simplicity was one of their main concerns.

In his essay on Thomas Ellwood, Whittier writes of the Journals:

> Little . . . can be said, as a general thing of their literary merits. Their authors were plain, earnest men and women, chiefly intent

upon the substance of things, and having withal a strong testimony
to bear against carnal wit and outside show and ornament. Yet,
even the scholar may well admire the power of certain portions
of George Fox's Journal, where a strong spirit clothes its utterance
in simple, downright Saxon words; the quiet and beautiful enthusiasm of Penington; the torrent energy of Edward Burrough;
the serene wisdom of Penn; the logical acuteness of Barclay; the
honest truthfulness of Sewell; the wit and humor of John Roberts,
(for even Quakerism had its apostolic jokers and drab-coated
Robert Halls); and last, not least, the simple beauty of Woolman's
Journal, the modest record of a life of good works and love (*Old
Portraits and Modern Sketches,* p. 35).

Journals, except for a few modern ones, were not published
during the lifetime of the writer. Many were not published at
all. Some manuscripts are kept in attics as family heirlooms,
like the Journal of Barclay White, an Indian Agent (1821-1906).
Some manuscripts repose in the vaults of historical libraries,
like that of Ann Warder (1758?-1829). Some, too long to be
published in their entirety, may be published in sections. Two
books have been made from parts of the diary of Elizabeth
Drinker (1734-1807). *Hannah Logan's Courtship,* edited by
Albert Cook Myers (Philadelphia: Ferris & Leach, 1904), is taken
from the long Journal of John Smith (1722-1771).

Some Journals are collections of letters, such as those of Sarah
Grubb (1756-1790) and Samuel Fothergill (1715-1772). *Sally
Wister's Journal* (1761-1804) is made up of her letters to Deborah Logan during the American Revolution. Deborah Logan's
seventeen volume diary has been abridged by Barbara Hopkins
Jones. A copy of the condensation is available in the Haverford
College Library. Some Journals are printed in the form of
diaries, like that of Dr. Rutty (1698-1775). The detailed information in many others indicates that they were originally compiled from diaries, sometimes by the children of the writer.
Often biographical material was added.

When a manuscript was found by the family, it was usually
turned over to a committee of the meeting for editing. This was
often disastrous. Sometimes the editors, from too much caution,
would eliminate references to persons then living, or other interesting parts of the Journal. About a hundred pages not found

in the printed edition of the Journal of Elias Hicks (1738-1830) are now in the Friends' Historical Library at Swarthmore College. The first edition of George Fox's Journal was edited by Thomas Ellwood, at one time Milton's secretary and reader. Ellwood was over-cautious in omitting Fox's self-praise and any references to his "miracles." The Journal was being published at a time when the Quakers were trying hard to become respectable. Since Fox's Journal stops in 1675, Ellwood made up the last fifteen years from biographical fragments and from letters. The edition of 1952 was completed instead with a chapter entitled "George Fox's Later Years" written by Henry Cadbury.

William Bacon Evans, himself a very Orthodox Friend, once told me with a smile that the editors of the Journal of Richard Jordan (1756-1826) had added some Orthodox sentiments not in the original. We have in print, at last, unabridged editions of the two best known Journals, those of John Woolman (edited by Amelia Mott Gummere, 1922)[1] and George Fox (edited by John L. Nickalls, 1952).

Two collections of Friends' writings were published in America after the separation of 1827, one by the Orthodox[2] and one by the Hicksites. About ninety Journals, some abbreviated, are contained in the fourteen volumes of the Friends' Library (Philadelphia: 1837-1850) edited by the Orthodox Friends, William and Thomas Evans. (The abbreviation F.L. will be used to indicate this collection.) It is reported that when the latest volume of the Friends' Library was delivered in the country districts of 19th century America, the farm bell was rung. Job Scott's Journal was omitted from this collection because he was not Orthodox, although he was one of the most popular preachers of his time.

The Friends' Miscellany (12 vols., Philadelphia: 1831-1839) is, according to the title page, a "collection of Essays and Fragments, Biographical, Religious, Epistolary, Narrative, and Historical" to preserve manuscripts "which may be useful to survivors." The editors, John and Isaac Comly, members of the

---

[1] Phillips Moulton has published a new edition of the Journal (Oxford University Press, 1971).

[2] Explanation of terms "Orthodox," "Hicksite," and "separation" appear in the final chapter.

body once called "Hicksite," also published the works of Job
Scott and Joshua Evans. (The Hicksites at the time of the
separation republished the works of George Fox and William
Penn to show that Hicks and his followers were in accord with
the founders.)

I have known personally the following writers of Journals:
Allen Jay, James Henderson, Elbert Russell, Stephen Hobhouse,
Corder Catchpool, Alfred Garrett, Rufus Jones, Inazo Nitobe,
Charles Darlington, William Hubben, Isaac Sharpless, and
Florence Sanville. A recent autobiographical book by Elizabeth
Vining, entitled *Quiet Pilgrimage* (Philadelphia: Lippincott,
1970), is one of the most recent "Journals" to appear, although
the author has told me that she had no intention of writing a
Journal. As she is still living, it is incomplete. Levi Pennington's
book entitled *Rambling Recollections of Ninety Happy Years*
(Newberg, Oregon: 1967) and Herbert Hoover's *Memoirs* (New
York: Macmillan, 1951-2) should at least be mentioned. Although
Unforgotten Years (London: Constable, 1938) by Logan Pearsall Smith (1865-1946) cannot be classified exactly as a spiritual
autobiography, it has unusual interest. He was "converted" at
an early age by a sister who later married Bernard Berenson,
and his parents were very active among Orthodox Friends in
Philadelphia and England. (His other sister was married to
Bertrand Russell.)

One of my favorite Quaker Journals is that of Caroline Fox
(1819-1871)—not related to George—entitled *Memories of Old
Friends* (Philadelphia: Lippincott, 1882). Her life does not fit
into the stages outlined in this book. She was an intimate friend
of the literary lights of her time, of whom there were many.
These include Wordsworth, Thomas and Jane Carlyle, Tenny-
son, Samuel and Hartley Coleridge, and especially John Stuart
Mill and his brother who died at the Fox home. I shall mention
only two brief incidents from her Journal:

> On one occasion Coleridge was holding forth on the effects pro-
> duced by his preaching, and appealed to Lamb, "You have heard
> me preach, I think?" "I have never heard you do anything else,"
> was the reply.
>
> J. Pease gave us a curious enough account of a shelf in the Ox-
> ford Library which is the receptacle of all works opposed to the

Church of England, which are placed there to be answered as way may open. Barclay's *Apology*, and Barclay's *Apology* alone, remains unanswered and unanswerable, though many times has it been taken from the shelf controversial, yet has always quietly slunk back to its old abode. Hurrah for Quakerism! (*Jour.*, 1882, pp. 14, 20).

The latest Quaker biography to come to the attention of the present writer is that of Roger Clark (Percy Lovell, *Quaker Inheritance, 1871-1961.* London: Bannisdale, 1970). It is compiled principally from autobiographical items.

Most of the Journals which I shall consider here were written before 1800. After 1800, about the time when Stephen Grellet discovered that Elias Hicks held "heretical" opinions, the Society of Friends was so uncertain about what it believed that it was thrown into complete confusion. For that reason, and because the custom of keeping a daily diary has declined, fewer Journals have appeared in the 19th and 20th centuries.

I am omitting a consideration of the Journals of the professional leaders of revival meetings, the fundamentalist Evangelistic Friends of the 19th century (such as that of Nathan and Esther Frame, Cleveland, Ohio: 1907). Their experience was quite different from that of the founders of the Society of Friends.

The Quaker religious autobiographies are all here referred to as "Journals," abbreviated *Jour.* The date of the edition used is cited. Their titles are often too long to quote. (They are cited in full in the bibliography. Often the word "Memoir" or "Life" or "Diary" appears in the title, but the term "Journal" is sufficiently general to include them all. Some "Journals" are partly biographical and partly autobiographical, such as those of Elizabeth Fry (Philadelphia: Vol. 1, 1847; Vol. II, 1848) and Daniel Wheeler (London: 1859), though Wheeler's South Pacific diary was published in a separate volume in 1840. When the "Journal" is not an autobiography, the fact is mentioned. Three exceptions to the autobiographical norm are the life of Isaac Hopper by L. Maria Child, the biography of John Roberts by his son Daniel, and the biography of Philip and Rachel Price by their son Eli. The dates of the birth and death of the various Journal writers are given in the text; they also appear in the bibliography for easy reference.

CHAPTER I

Characteristics of the Quaker Journalists

QUAKER simplicity included simplicity in writing. Friends avoided ornate writing much as they avoided ornate dress and furniture. Personal experiences, except those which concerned their religion, were seldom referred to. A dream is mentioned if it is thought to be significant. Experiences in early childhood are mentioned if they are thought to have religious meaning. I can think of only two Journalists who describe their courtship and marriage: David Ferris and Thomas Ellwood. Few mention the birth and death of their children, except when such an event had a special religious significance.

Humorous stories are told about Quakers who went to extraordinary lengths to tell the exact truth. A good story can be spoiled by too much truth. Edward Hicks (1780-1849) confesses in his Journal that, as he was an artist, he gave way to putting too much color in his stories. (*Memoirs*, 1851, p. 72) John Comly (1773-1850) opens his Journal with these words: "According to the account given by my parents, I was born the 19th day of the 11th month, 1773." (*Jour.*, 1853, p. 3)

In addition to the necessity for simplicity and truth was the requirement of humility. It is difficult to write about oneself and, at the same time, be humble. John Woolman (1720-1772) produced three versions of his Journal in an effort to eliminate as much as possible the pronoun "I." John Rutty (1698-1775), author of several famous medical books, was so hard on himself that the editors of his diary wrote a preface to say that he was a much better man than he said he was.

The problem of pride can be avoided by attributing all achievements to God. No Quaker would dare congratulate a Quaker minister on his sermon. The most he should say is, "Thee was favored." I once heard, in my own meeting, a stranger say to Thomas Whitson, "Thee preached a fine sermon today, Thomas." "Yes," replied Thomas, "the devil told me that just as I was sitting down."

The Journalists do not mention the subjects on which they preached except in a few cases. The subject of the first sermon is often mentioned, as it was usually very short and marked an important milestone in spiritual progress.

All of the Quaker Journalists had a theology, but this is rarely mentioned or mentioned only indirectly. They were less ortho- dox by Puritan standards than they themselves recognized. The Puritans knew, better than the Quakers did, how unorthodox Quakers were and, accordingly, subjected them to a long and very savage persecution. As the Quakers were pacifists, they met this persecution by patient non-resistance. More than four hundred died in the filthy English dungeons. Their sufferings were particularly severe because they would not bribe the jailers to give them food and bedding. Besse's *Collection of the Suffer- ings of the People Called Quakers* (London: 1753) contains about 20,000 names. But there is little mention of this suffering or persecution in the Journals.

The controversy was continued in America between the Quak- ers in the middle colonies and the Puritans in New England. In New England four Quakers were hanged on Boston Common and many others were treated with great brutality. It is a strange fact that historians of America attribute the conception of re- ligious freedom to the Puritans and not to the Quakers. In New England only the Puritans could vote, but in the Quaker col- onies all could vote. Since the Puritans had as their spokesmen professional ministers especially trained to express their beliefs and the Quakers had no professional preachers, historians have much ignored the Quaker contribution to the thought and prac- tice of the American colonies.

The Quaker spiritual autobiographies are quite different from those written by the Puritans. Anyone who thinks that Quaker- ism is simply a more extreme form of Puritanism should notice this. The Puritans believed in predestination, and their salvation depended on a divine monarch who could, without good reason, consign them forever to hell. The Puritan could not save himself, so he watched desperately for evidence of divine grace. In the diaries of John Bunyan, Increase and Cotton Mather, Jonathan Edwards, and others, we find an extreme anxiety, interrupted only occasionally by a brief discovery of grace. The possibility of not being elected and the impossibility of doing anything about it, drove some Puritans literally insane.

At the Salem witch trials the judges and the "witches" were obviously out of their minds. Nothing like this happened in Pennsylvania. At one trial at which a "witch" had been acquitted by a jury, she was asked by Penn if she could travel through the air on a broomstick. When she said, "Yes," Penn replied, "I know of no law against it." A Quaker who was disowned by his meeting for consulting a soothsayer in trying to find a lost horse, apologized and was restored to membership.

In contrast to the extreme anxiety exhibited by the Puritan diarists, we find in the Quaker Journals accounts of complete inward peace for long periods.

Elizabeth Stirredge (1634-1706), raised in a Puritan household, records in her Journal, addressed to her children, how as a child she had suffered from fear of hell and damnation. She writes:

> In my tender years I was one of a sad heart, and much concerned and surprized with inward fear what would become of me when I should die: and when my lot was to be near any that would talk rudely, or swear, or be overcome with strong drink, I dreaded to pass by them; and when I heard it thunder, oh the dread and terror that would fall upon me; and I could get the most private place that I could to mourn in secret, thinking the Lord would render vengeance upon the heads of the wicked. When I saw the flashes of lightning, oh, thought I, whither shall I go to hide myself from the wrath of the dreadful and terrible God. . . . Oh! what would I have parted with for the enjoyment of the Lord, and assurance of salvation.
>
> (*Jour.*, 1810, pp. 23, 25)

After hearing William Dewsbury, one of the best of the early Quaker preachers, she records her release from fear.

> Oh, he was one that had good tidings for me in that day, and great power was with his testimony at that very time; for the hardness was taken away, and my heart was opened.
>
> (*Jour.*, 1810, p. 41)

A sense of inward peace is especially mentioned after some difficult concern has been carried out, whether successfully or not. The first sermon in meeting was usually preceded by a long struggle to overcome the reluctance to appear in public. There is always a mention afterward of inward peace.

Historians have called the prominent Quakers of the 18th century "quietists." This does not mean that they were quiet. Their Journals indicate that they were anything but quiet when they felt a concern to act. They were "quietists" only in the sense that they tried to quiet all selfish desires and motives in order to devote themselves without any reservation to the concern they felt.

When Daniel Wheeler felt called upon to take a long voyage in the South Pacific, he experienced anxiety at the prospect. When Thomas Shillitoe felt called upon to hold Quaker meetings in about a thousand Irish drinking houses, he experienced a sleepless night before each setting out. But in each case the concern was carried out.

The Quaker meeting for worship and the Quaker meeting for business are unique institutions. It is their purpose to expose the soul to the Light from God so that peace is removed if it ought to be removed, or attained if it can be attained. If the soul becomes sensitive, if its vision is widened and deepened so that new areas of life come within its ken, then a new requirement may be laid upon it and peace removed until that requirement is met. If the soul is able to find in the silence union with the peace of God at the heart of existence, then inward peace is secured and new knowledge and power received.

In spite of the great differences among the Journals as each expresses the individuality of the writer, they all record similar stages of development. These stages result from the character of the Quaker religion, not from the imitation of earlier Journals. The Quaker stages are: divine revelations in childhood, remembered by some but not all of the Journalists. Then a period of youthful playfulness which is, unfortunately, looked back

upon as a waste of time. This period is followed by an experience of a divided self, in which the writer is preparing to devote his whole life to following the Light. After that inner conflict, the leadings of the Light are followed as much as the
spiritual capacity of the writer permits. This capacity may vary
considerably. When the Journalist stands up in meeting to speak
for the first time, an important milestone in his career is passed.
Another important milestone is the adoption of the so-called
"plain" dress and other Quaker customs requiring sincerity and
the absence of all superfluities. The soul, no longer exhausting
its energy in conflict with itself, becomes integrated and uni-
fied. Hence arises new power and vision for tasks ahead.

CHAPTER II

Divine Revelations in Childhood

THE TIMES of innocence" are often recorded in journals which aim at completeness. William Caton (1636-1665) wrote in the first Journal to be published:

> While I was yet very young . . . being inspired with a divine principle, I did in those days sometimes feel the power of it overcoming my heart.
>
> *(Jour.* F. L. IX: 435)

He set a style which was generally followed.

"In my early age I was sensible of the tender impressions of divine love" is a typical expression as written by Mary Hagger (1758-1840) *(Jour.* F.L. VII: 432). The age of seven to twelve seems to have been the usual time for such divine visitations. At the time these were not always recognized for what they were.

In the Journal of his travels in Holland and Germany, William Penn (1644-1718) describes a meeting with the Labadists who were looking for "a more spiritual fellowship and society."

> Here I began to let them know how, and when, the Lord first appeared unto me, which was about the twelfth year of my age, anno 1656. How at times, betwixt that and the fifteenth, the Lord visited me, and the divine impressions he gave me of himself.
>
> *(Select Works,* London: 1771, p. 478)

On some occasion Penn must have described this first experience more fully. We have this report in the biography by Thomas Clarkson:

> While here (at Chigwell school) and alone in his chamber, being

then eleven years old, he was suddenly surprised with an inward comfort and as he thought an external glory in the room, which gave rise to religious emotions, during which he had the strongest conviction of the being of a God, and that the soul of man was capable of enjoying communication with him. He believed also that the seal of Divinity had been put upon him at this moment, or that he had been awakened or called upon to a holy life.

(Memoirs of the Private and Public Life
of William Penn. Philadelphia: 1814, I:5-6)

William Penn grew up in an atmosphere of political and ideological tension between the Puritans and the Church of England. Mary Penington (1625-1682), mother of Penn's first wife, says that her parents were "a kind of loose Protestants." When, at the age of ten or eleven, she went to live with "some that appeared to be more religious," she "began to be very serious about religion."

One day, after we came from the place of public worship, the maid . . . read one of Preston's sermons, the text was: "Pray continually." In this sermon much was said respecting prayer: amongst other things, of the excellency of prayer, that it distinguished a saint from a sinner; that in many things the hypocrite could imitate the saint, but in this he could not. This thing wrought much on my mind. I found that I knew not what true prayer was; for what I used for prayer, an ungodly person could use as well as I, which was to read one out of a book, and this could not be the prayer he meant, which distinguished a saint from a wicked one. My mind was deeply exercised about this thing. When she had done reading, and all were gone out of the chamber, I shut the door, and in great distress I flung myself on the bed, and oppressedly cried out: "Lord, what is prayer?"

(Jour. Philadelphia: Biddle Press, p. 19)

She tried writing some prayers of her own, but it was not until she was about thirteen years old that she could say:

I was unable to sit at my work, but was strongly inclined to go into a private room, which I did, and shutting the door, kneeled down and poured out my soul to the Lord in a very vehement manner. I was wonderfully melted and eased, and felt peace and acceptance with the Lord: and that this was true prayer, which I had never before been acquainted with.

(Ibid., p. 22)

The parents of John Crook (1627-1699) saw to it that he was "instructed in their way [Church of England]" until he was ten or eleven years old,

> within which time, I had many exercises in my inward man, and often prayed in by-corners, as words sprang in my mind, and as I learned prayers without book; yet many strong combatings remained within me. . . . I was almost overcome to consent, the devil urging me thereunto by a mighty violent striving, to run down all my resistance and withstanding of him. But on a sudden, there arose in me a power and life that did oppose and gainsay the enemy, making my spirit say within me, with much boldness and courage, I will not serve thee, O satan, but I will serve the Lord God of heaven and earth, whatsoever I suffer, or becometh of me therefor. . . . By the ease and relief I found in my inward parts, I concluded it was the Lord who helped me in so great a strait.
>
> *(Jour.,* F. L. XIII:207)

The mother of Benjamin Bangs (1652-1741) was the daughter of an Anglican clergyman, but she had seen "so much deceit and hypocrisy covered under the pretense of religion" that she became a convinced Friend when her son was about fifteen years old. He recalled in his Journal:

> When I was between eleven and twelve years of age, I was much given to divert myself in running, wrestling, and foot-ball playing. . . . Being one day by myself, not far from the place of our habitation, I met with such a visitation, as I had been altogether ignorant of before, in which a sweet calmness spread over my mind; and it rose in my heart, that if I could but keep to this, what might I grow up to in time?
>
> *(Jour.,* F. L. IV:215)

His mother was very happy to hear about this, though Benjamin himself did not become a Quaker until he was nineteen or twenty.

Joseph Pike (1657-1729), on the other hand, was born to parents who were already Friends. His father, while in the army in Ireland, had found that "for conscience' sake, he could not use arms for the destruction of mankind. He was turned out of the army, after which he betook himself to a country life." His son relates:

Before I was seven years of age, the Spirit of the Lord began to work in my mind, and strove with me, to bring me off from childish playfulness and vanities. . . . Though I did not presently know, that it was the Lord's Spirit which I felt working in me, as Samuel knew not the Lord's voice, when a child, yet being convinced in myself, by its holy convictions, that I ought not to do those things which brought trouble upon me, and also, that when at any time I refrained from doing what caused this trouble, I had sweet peace and satisfaction of mind . . . whereby, I grew into sobriety beyond many of my age, until I came to be about nine years old.

(Jour., F. L. II:357)

By the beginning of the nineteenth century, a Quaker Journalist might be descended from a long line of birthright Friends. Samuel Janney (1801-1880) was such a one. He wrote:

I remember that at a very early age I experienced the operation of divine grace condemning me for evil, and inciting me to goodness. . . . When I read the narratives of the Evangelists concerning the discourses and miracles of Christ, I sometimes thought if I had only lived at the time when he was personally on earth, how gladly would I have followed in his footsteps. . . . But I have since learned that we of this generation are as high favored as any that have lived before us . . . we may have access to the Father through the son, by obedience to the manifestations of his light and grace in our hearts . . . and . . . we live in an age and country where we enjoy civil and religious liberty.

(Jour., 1881, p. 6)

Rufus Jones (1863-1948) describes family meeting in his home before he was old enough to go to school.

The silences, during which all the children of our family were hushed with a kind of awe, were very important features of my spiritual development. There was work inside and outside the house waiting to be done, and yet we sat there hushed and quiet, doing nothing. I very quickly discovered that something *real* was taking place. We were feeling our way down to that place from which living words come and very often they did come. Some one would bow and talk with God so simply and quietly that He never seemed far away. The words helped to explain the silence. We were now finding what we had been searching for. When I first began to think of God I did not think of Him as very far off.

(*Finding the Trail of Life*. 1929, pp. 21-22)

Early Journalists who grew up in a Puritan environment, like Elizabeth Stirredge, quoted in chapter I (p. 3), were often concerned about the doctrine of original sin. John Churchman (1705-1775) felt that his parents' taking him to Friends' Meeting helped him in this respect:

> I early felt reproof for bad words and actions, yet knew not whence it came, until about the age of eight years, as I sat in a small meeting, the Lord by his heavenly love and goodness, overcame and tendered my heart, and by his glorious light discovered to me the knowledge of himself. .... I was early taught to think differently from such who hold the perdition of infants, and am since confirmed in believing that the sin of our first parents is not imputed to us.
>
> (*Jour*. 1882, pp. 7-8)

It is a Quaker doctrine that all persons young or old have at least the seed of the Inward Light, though the seed or germ may not have grown yet. No Puritan could have said, as Churchman did: "Blessed for ever be the name of the Lord! who in his infinite mercy and goodness clearly informed me, that if I would mind the discoveries of his Truth, and pure Light for the future, what I had done in the time of my ignorance, he would wink at and forgive." *(Ibid.)*

The Puritans considered children totally depraved, just as they considered adherents of non-Christian religions to be totally depraved. They treated the American Indian as a child of the devil. The Quaker considered non-Christian religions as immature religions, containing an element of truth which can be developed further. One scholar of religions, Max Moeller, has said that a primitive religion is no more a false religion than a child is a false man.

The contrast between the Puritan and the Quaker views of immature religion, whether of non-Christians or of children, is clear in the contrast between Milton and Whittier. In *Paradise Lost* Milton depicts Satan's army as officered by heathen deities. The battles between the armies of Jehovah and Satan are fought in a spirit of the Old Testament and not the New. The victor displays no love or forgiveness.

In *The Shadow and the Light* Whittier explains:

> All souls that struggle and aspire,
> All hearts of prayer by Thee are lit;
> And, dim or clear, Thy tongues of fire
> On dusky tribes and twilight centuries sit.
>
> Nor bounds, nor clime, nor creed thou know'st,
> Wide as our need thy favors fall;
> The white wings of the Holy Ghost
> Stoop, seen or unseen, o'er the heads of all.

The Quaker Journalists who recorded their childhood revelations were exceptional persons in the degree of their later dedication to their religion and in sensitivity to the Inward Light. It is not surprising that genius in religion, like genius in other lines, should display itself in childhood. According to Dr. Catharine Cox (Miles) in her study *The Early Mental Traits of Three Hundred Geniuses* (Stanford University Press, 1926): "Later achievement was foreshadowed in youthful behavior, and it is probable that early manifestations of superior intelligence could have been found in every case had the records all been faithfully kept." (p. 217) The recording of early religious experience in the Quaker Journals may have been influenced by the Quaker belief that God is never at any age or place without His witness in the heart.

Experience in attempting to teach children leads me to believe that Quaker training can contribute a great deal to the development of this sensitivity. Students in the school where I began teaching had not had such training. The "seeds of Divine goodness" within them had definitely not been encouraged to germinate. Then I went to teach at a genuinely Quaker school where the children had been brought up in Quaker meetings and homes. At the Friends' School near Barnesville, Ohio, the students were well advanced in Christian beliefs and in the Christian religion. The "discipline problem" was not even thought of there.

Some of the Quaker Journalists record turning points in their early lives that were a result of training rather than divine revelation. Benjamin Hallowell (1799-1877) records such a point. At the age of eight he dreaded going to school because of the severity of the teacher.

> One morning, under a strong pressure of these feelings, I thought I would make one more effort, and hide my hat. When the time arrived to go to school, mother brought me my basket of dinner and said, "Now, my son, it is time to go to school." I told her I could not see my hat anywhere. She told me to look again. I replied, I had been looking a long time. She then came to assist me in hunting it, and whether or not she suspected I had hidden it, I never knew; but she went deliberately and got her black silk bonnet, and said, "Thee can wear this to-day," and without changing a muscle of her face, began to tie it on, I looking steadily into her eye, where, child as I was, I could see a look of determination that I knew to be irresistible. I exclaimed, "Oh, mother, I *think* I can find my hat" (but she kept on tying the strings of the bonnet); "I am *sure* I can find it, mother, it is in the dough-trough," by which time the bonnet was well tied on and her countenance still unrelaxed. This circumstance is strongly impressed on me to this day. I went with a quick step to the dough-trough and got my hat, and said, "Here it is, mother; please take this bonnet off," which she did, to my great joy, and I felt that I had made a narrow escape, and never tried it again. This was one turning point in my life.

> *(Jour.* 1883, pp. 7-8)

In my early youth I went regularly to Meeting before my feet could reach the floor when I was seated. The preaching was a mixture of Biblical texts, set to a chant like the Gregorian.* It produced in me a sense of solemnity. It was definitely religious, not secular in tone as are so many of the sermons in Meeting today.

In many Meetings the only religious education attempted is First Day School. Except for the singing of hymns, teaching in First Day school is so much like the teaching in the rest of the week that it has little religious effect. Alfred North Whitehead has said that it is one evidence of the vitality of the Christian religion that it has survived the Sunday school.

---

* See also: Joshua Baily, Jr. "Friends and Music," *Bulletin of the Friends' Historical Association.* XXIII (Spring, 1934), 21-30.

The Quaker Journalists were undoubtedly persons of unusual religious maturity. While children today are maturing much earlier physically and intellectually, their parents could still benefit from the advice of John Comly.

The incalculable advantages of taking little children to meetings, and of habituating them early to the discipline of stillness, can never be fully appreciated. It may be the means of laying a foundation, very early in life, for the most exalted virtues. The seeds of Divine goodness thus planted, or that germinate in good wishes and good desires, when the infant mind is thus retired, may take deep root and bring forth early fruits of genuine religion— of love and obedience to parents—of sincere affection toward brothers and sisters and relatives. Under these solemnizing, tender feelings, the pure, innocent, uncontaminated infant mind worships in spirit and in truth. It learns to love such opportunities —it delights to feel such a calmness and quietude—and it enjoys a heaven within.

(Jour. 1853, p. 4)

CHAPTER III

Youthful Frivolity

A PERIOD of youthful frivolity seems to have been a definite stage in the experience of nearly all the Journalists. The follies of this period, usually the years from ten to fifteen, though sometimes later, were generally attributed to the depravity of a "natural" disposition not yet aware of its shortcomings.

Accounts of such frivolity are all very much alike. Typical expressions are: "My mind was drawn out after vain plays, customs, fashions, and will worship of the world," (James Dickinson, 1659-1741: F. L. XII, 370); "The impetuous waves of youthful passion, too often carried the weak, wayward young man out of the straight narrow way," (Edward Hicks: *Memoirs,* 1851, p. 50); "The vivacity of my natural disposition often led me beyond natural bounds," (Sarah Hunt, 1797-1889: *Jour.,* 1892, p. 3); "I took great pleasure in airy and vain company," (David Ferris, 1707-1799: *Jour.,* 1855, p. 18. David Ferris wrote the first part of his Journal in Latin because he was so ashamed of his early behavior.)

No Journal records misdeeds more serious than "frothiness of behavior" and fondness for such things as sport, music, card playing, dancing, jesting, and "vain and loose conversation." Job Scott (1751-1793) is thankful that "the Lord preserved me from hard drinking though often in the way of temptation and solicitation to it. Swearing also I mostly refrained from." (*Jour.,* 1831, pp. 31-2). Hannah Taylor (1774-1812) speaks for all when she says, "I felt thankful that I had been preserved from gross

14

sins in the days of my youth, but I was convicted of much light-
ness and emptiness from having given way to the natural liveliness of my disposition." (*Jour.*, 1820, p. 6.)

One wonders whether those grave journalists would have been
the able persons they were had they not possessed this "natural
liveliness" which they so regretfully record. They were poor
psychologists if they did not know that childish playfulness is
a necessary preparation for life. In play the child develops skills
and attitudes which are necessary for successful mature life. But
if we look in the children's books of the 17th century, we find
that the children are depicted as small adults, not as being entirely different in body and mind.

We have given little space to this second period in the development of the Quaker Journalists. The accounts are not only
very similar in all the Journals. They also resemble closely the
experience of Puritans in their childhood. But the Quakers did
not consider the frivolous behavior sinful so much as a waste of
time.

Thomas Scattergood relates that while he was taking a sleigh
ride in Fairmount Park he was overcome by the feeling that he
was wasting his time and asked to be put down. Later while he
was yachting in the Delaware River he had the same remorse,
but of course he could not, as before, stop his ride.

Some diversions were considered more acceptable for young
Friends than others. Interest in science, particularly botany and
ornithology, took the place of interest in the arts for many
Quakers, principally because these sciences were concerned with
facts and not with products of the imagination. Between 1851
and 1900, writes A. Ruth Fry in *Quaker Ways* (London: Cas-
sell, 1933), a Quaker "had forty-six times more chance of election
as a Fellow of the Royal Society than his fellow countrymen"
(p. 206). Edward Cope (1840-1897) was started on his career as
a famous naturalist by his father. At the age of five he learned:

> Pigs have bristles,
> Cows have hair,
> Birds have feathers,
> Snakes are bare.

> (*Jour.*, 1931, p. 39)

I do not find in the Journals any justification of the former Quaker testimony against instrumental music. Thomas Clarkson, not himself a Quaker, states the cause of this testimony in *A Portraiture of Quakerism* (Philadelphia: James P. Parke, 1808):

> Music, again, if it were encouraged in the Society, would be considered as depriving those of maturer years of hours of comfort, which they now frequently enjoy, in the service of religion. Retirement is considered by the Quakers as a Christian duty. The members therefore, of this Society are expected to wait in silence, not only in their private places of worship, but occasionally in their families, or in their private chambers, in the intervals of their daily occupations, that, in stillness of heart and in freedom from the active contrivance of their own wills, they may acquire both directions and strength for the performance of the duties of life. The Quakers, therefore, are of opinion, that, if instrumental music were admitted as a gratification in leisure hours, it would take the place of many of these serious retirements, and become very injurious to their interests and their character as Christians.
>
> (I: 34-5)

To spend time in learning to play a musical instrument was considered frivolous. The objection to vocal music would not hold to the same extent. That there were objections, however, is very clear: John Comly refers to his "unbecoming noise" in attempting "to imitate singing as practised by vulgar or profane persons." (*Jour.*, 1853, p. 17)

Congregational singing was opposed more on the grounds of insincerity than frivolity. Words might be sung that would not be sincere expressions of the singer's feelings. When David Ferris was still a Presbyterian and "partook of their bread and wine," he did not feel free to sing with them, "not having been, for some time before, in a condition to sing; besides, it did not appear to me an acceptable sacrifice, or anything like divine worship, for a mixed multitude to sing that of which they knew nothing by experience." (*Jour.*, 1855, p. 35)

Singing by an individual, if guided by the Spirit, might be permitted. There are eight references in Fox's Journal which relate that he sang. Paul says, "I will sing with the spirit and I will sing with the mind also." (I Corinthians 14:15.) But the

Psalms were sung only in the outer court of the temple, not near the Holy of Holies. In a Quaker meeting house the First Day school room might be described as the "outer court," while the meeting for worship might be compared to the Holy of Holies. As the prophet says, "the Lord is in his holy temple: let all the earth keep silence before him." (Habakkuk, 2:20)

The writing of verse has never been considered as frivolous as music, although Catherine Phillips reports:

> Soon after I appeared in the ministry, I dropped my pen in regard to verses. I do not say it was a sacrifice required; but the continuing of the practice might have proved a snare some way: it might have engaged my attention too much, or tended to make me popular, which I have ever guarded against, perhaps too much so in some points.
>
> (*Jour.*, 1798, pp. 20-21)

Early poems are included in several Journals. Joel Bean (1825-1914) wrote a rhymed chronicle of his youth which includes a description of quarterly meeting in Dover, New Hampshire:

> The reunion of Friends was affectionate where
> The hearts were attuned to worship and prayer.
> Where the humblest home-toilers some offerings brought
> Of the fruits of the year's new experience and thought.
>
> Then the meeting house crowded, the solemnized throng
> Hearts tendered and quickened for duty more strong;
> The greetings of Friends and grasping of hands,
> And the sealed benediction the soul understands.
>
> ("Recollections of Childhood")

Occasional youthful playfulness can be found in any period of life as I know from my own experience with weighty Friends. The following story about Isaac Hopper (1771-1852) is a good example of Quaker humor.

> One day he went to a hosiery store, and said to the man, "I bought a pair of stockings here yesterday. They looked very nice; but when I got home, I found two large holes in them; and I have come for another pair." The man summoned his wife, and informed her of what the gentleman had said.
>
> "Bless me! Is it possible, sir?" she exclaimed.

"Yes," replied Friend Hopper, "I found they had holes as large as my hand."

"It is very strange," rejoined she; "for I am sure they were new. But if you have brought them back, of course we will change them."

"O," said he, "upon examination, I concluded that the big holes were made to put the feet in; and I liked the stockings so well, that I have come to buy another pair."

(Jour., 1853, p. 366)

CHAPTER IV

The Divided Self

THE PERIOD of childish frivolity—usually about the time of adolescence—merges into the period of inward tension which continues until the Inward Light is accepted as the guide of life. This does not mean that the guidance of the Light is accepted only as an idea received from parents or preachers. Rather it becomes an integral and integrating part of life.

For some Friends the change from frivolity to inward guidance is so smooth that no inward struggle occurs, but for most the prize must be fought for and won. That so few in the 17th and 18th centuries escaped this inward tension may be a result of the theology of that time. In the 19th century this struggle appears only in a mild form; sometimes not at all.

The expectation of a struggle between the flesh and the spirit results from some of the writings of Paul. In Romans 7:15-20 Paul gives us a vivid description of his inward struggle.

> I do not understand my own actions. For I do not do what I want, but I do the very thing I hate. Now if I do what I do not want, I agree that the law is good. So then it is no longer I that do it, but sin which dwells within me. For I know that nothing good dwells within me, that is, in my flesh. I can will what is right, but I cannot do it. For I do not do the good I want, but the evil I do not want is what I do. Now if I do what I do not want, it is no longer I that do it, but sin which dwells within me.

The Puritans believed that the struggle was lifelong. The Westminster Confession of Faith declares that even the saints continue to sin in body, mind, and spirit ceaselessly. But they

19

have ignored the 8th chapter of Romans where Paul declares that Christ in him wins the victory: "But if Christ is in you, although your bodies are dead because of sin, your spirits are alive because of righteousness." (Romans 8:10)

That the Puritans found their religion a source of continuous anxiety while the Quakers found their religion a source of inward peace may be partly due to the fact that, for the Puritans, salvation, the atonement of Christ, heaven and hell, are all external and therefore uncertain. The battle for man's soul is won only by a free gift of grace, undeserved, as man is depraved because of Adam's fall. Man can only be sure of what is internal and therefore directly experienced. The internal struggle for complete submission to the Inward Light is described in many of the Journals.

Most Quaker Journalists speak of a divided self before the final integration of the soul occurs. This is not a result of a dualistic theology so much as a consequence of experience. The Journal writer remembers a time when he felt two forces acting upon him, one pulling up and the other down. The animal fleshly force pulls down and the spiritual force pulls up. This dualistic philosophy was almost universal in Christian sects before the 19th century. After 1800 a monistic theology occasionally appears which permits the writer to pass smoothly into a higher condition.

In *Varieties of Religious Experience* William James calls the monistic type the "healthy minded" and the dualistic the "sick soul." The sick soul is more common in Quaker Journals; inner peace and unity are worth more if they are achieved after a struggle.

St. Augustine gives in his *Confessions* a long and detailed account of his struggles. He aptly compares his condition to a person who wakes up in the morning. His animal nature persuades him to stay in bed; his spiritual nature urges him to get up. The divided self is a natural condition that usually results only in uncertainty. But this condition can be serious when the salvation of the soul is involved or the significance or meaning of life is concerned.

The period of search and conflict follows the discovery of something in the soul that is not satisfied by "youthful frivolity."

It may look back to a childhood revelation of divinity. This period generally lasts from the middle teens to the early twenties. There is much variation and in some cases conflict never ceases. In others, more often women than men, this conflict is felt only slightly.

With the Friends of the 17th century the period of conflict was often associated with a period of searching out various preachers and sects in an effort to attain release from the inner struggle. The conflict is described in very much the same terms in all the Journals from the earliest to the latest. The seventh chapter of Romans, in which Paul writes of his own inner conflicts, furnished terms in which some described these battles fought in the depths of the soul. John Barclay (1797-1838) quotes:

> . . . how to perform that which is good, I find not; for the good that I would, I do not; but the evil which I would not, that do I.
> (*Jour.*, 1877, p. 23)

Metaphors from the Old Testament also helped Journalists to express their conflicts:

> A long wilderness had to be passed through before I could enjoy the land of promise. . . . I believe it is impossible for any mortal to understand or conceive the depth and intensity of these mental conflicts without having personally experienced some of them.
> (George Richardson, 1773-1863.
> *Jour.*, 1856, pp. xvi, xviii)

> As I was careful to keep in the Light I came to see the kingdom rent from Saul and given to David though there was a long war between the house of Saul and the house of David.
> (James Dickinson, *Jour.*, F. L. XII:370)

Other typical expressions of conflict are:

> Oh, the many days of sorrow and nights of deep distress that I passed through as I lay wallowing in the filthiness of the flesh.
> (Rebecca Jones, 1739-1818, *Jour.*, 1849, p. 6)

> But the enemy who is ever near to damp the good in us, troubled me with many of his suggestions, that it could never be the way to attain happiness, to discharge myself of the worship due to God

for his favors; yet the more I gave way to the thoughts of flinging myself on the mercy of God, the more also I found a hope to spring within my soul, that the Lord would point out a way for me. This drew me still further from all ceremonies, and gave my mind such a turn from those diversions I once took delight in, that my uncle and aunt took notice of it, and called it melancholy.

(Margaret Lucas, 1701-1769. Jour., 1803, p. 19)

Job Scott, reproved by his father and aware that he was acting in "opposition to the dictates of the holy spirit . . . strove to stifle the witness and persuade (himself) there was no harm" in running "into company," dancing and playing cards.

Thus I went on frolicking and gaming, and spending my precious time in vanity. Often at night, or in the night, and sometimes near the break of day, I have returned home from my merry meetings grievously condemned, distressed, and ashamed; wishing I had not gone into such company, and resolving to do so no more; but soon my resolution failed me, and away I went again and again; and thus continued making still greater strides in folly than before. . . . Sometimes when I have stood upon the floor to dance, with a partner by the hand, before all were quite ready, God has arisen in judgement, and smitten me to the very heart . . . but resolutely mustering all the stoutness I was master of, I brazened it out until the music called me to the dance, and then I soon drowned the voice of conviction, became merry, and caroused among my companions in dissipation, until time urged a dismission of our jovial assembly. . . . I have not forgotten those sad and, mournful walks, at the conclusion of my midnight revellings, I . . . have come to a full stand, stopped and sat down on a stump, stone, or log, by the way, wrung my hands, and strewed my tears before the Lord, in sorrow and extremity of anguish, bordering almost on desperation. . . . Sometimes I spent near all the first-day of the week, when I should have been at meeting, in playing cards, idle if not dissolute conversation, and other vain amusements, returning home at night in condemnation, and sometimes sighing and crying.   (Jour., 1831, pp. 29-31)

He had an interesting dream that foreshadowed the end of his conflict. (See page 96 below.)

This inward conflict, or "tossed state," is often described as the conflict between two "wills," "powers," or "seeds" in the soul.

I had never had before such a clear and undoubted sense of the
two powers of light and life and death and darkness.

(William Evans, 1787-1867. *Jour.*, 1870 p. 17)

John Whitehead (1630-1696) makes this conflict the subject of
his autobiographical pamphlet *The Enmity between the Two
Seeds: wherein is discovered the subtilty and envie of the Serpent's Seed: who rules in the Man of Sin, that is born after the
flesh, and persecutes him that is born after the Spirit; which
spiritual birth is here witnessed (by the operation of the power
of God, through much travel) of the immortal Seed, which was
promised, and is come to bruise the Serpent's Head, and discover him in all his Wiles, where he appears.* (London: 1655)
(Joseph Smith, *A Descriptive Catalog of Friends' Books.* London: 1867, II:909).

C. G. Jung in his writings, which are concerned with the integration or individuation of the self, has ably described the
psychological characteristics and explanations of this condition.
We need not consider a cleft in the soul as an exceptional or
necessarily a pathological condition. Such divided states are the
common lot of all persons in varying degrees; no personality is
fully integrated. The Quaker Journalists were educated in a
dualistic theology with a sharp distinction between natural and
supernatural. Theology undoubtedly had a considerable influence upon the course as well as upon the interpretation of
their inner experiences. They faced a problem common to all
men which took on desperate seriousness because of an unusually
persistent determination to solve it. Who indeed has not faced
some conflict between the will to do good and the will to do
evil, and found himself quite unable to reach a solution through
his own power?

Whether it be interpreted as a conflict between God and Satan
for possession of the human soul as Bunyan depicts it in *Holy
War,* or a conflict between the "natural" earthly part of man
and a divinely inspired Light within, or a conflict between a
lower and higher self, or between a conscious and subconscious
personality, it is in any case a very real thing. A religious group
which has discovered a solution has made a definite contribution to the happiness of mankind.

Only through real conflict can real spiritual depth be won. Catherine Phillips writes:

> I have it as an observation that I have seldom, if ever, seen any stand and arrive to any considerable degree of usefulness in the Church, whose foundation has not been deeply laid in afflictions and exercises.
>
> *(Jour.,* 1798, p. 19)

And these afflictions, for the Journalists, were not to be avoided.

> I tried many ways to flee from him, but he followed me up as he did the children of Israel in their travels.
>
> (Thomas Arnett, 1791-1877. *Jour.,* 1884, p. 19)

They felt like Francis Thompson pursued by the Hound of Heaven:

> I fled Him, down the nights and down the days;
>   I fled Him, down the arches of the years;
> I fled Him, down the labyrinthine ways
>   Of my own mind; and in the mist of tears
> I hid from Him, and under running laughter.
>   . . .
>   But with unhurrying chase,
>   And unperturbed pace,
> Deliberate speed, majestic instancy,
>   . . .
>   Came on the following Feet,
>   And a Voice above their beat—
>   . . .
> "All things betray thee, who betrayest Me."
>
> (from verses 1 and 2)

CHAPTER V

Unification Through Silence

I T IS HOPED that this chapter may be useful to individuals and meetings on the growing edge of Quakerism because, though the 20th century differs radically from the 17th, the methods by which the Society of Friends is growing today do not differ essentially from those of the earliest times. The opportunities open to the founders of the Society of Friends are open to us now, and their methods are still applicable.

This study may also be useful to readers who are not Friends but who are interested in religion based on inward life and in the history of religion, particularly that much misunderstood form called mysticism.

Mysticism is an element in every form of religion. The Quaker Journals or spiritual autobiographies quoted here are as valuable a source of material on the history and nature of mysticism as are the writings of many more widely known mystics.

Historians, if they notice Quakerism at all, tend to neglect what might be called its inner side. This is not surprising because the inner side is subjective and largely incommunicable. In early America, Quakers at one time or another governed five of the colonies: Pennsylvania, New Jersey, Rhode Island, Delaware, and, for a short time, North Carolina, where they lost their political power because they refused the required oath for office holders. The result of the Quaker movement cannot be understood without reference to the inward experiences out of which their equalitarian and democratic ideas arose. The great, but almost hidden, influence of the Quaker movement on early

25

America is described by Henry Seidel Canby (editor of the *Saturday Review* 1924-1939):

> The mental habits and ideals of the Quakers are stronger in the American mind today than anything else that has been brought over seas and only to be equalled by the effect of the native environment itself. . . . We know that Penn's State was the first model of a liberal government and far closer in ideals and practice to our United States than was the Puritan theocracy. But it is too commonly supposed that essential Quakerism was lost in the rigidity which strangled the Friends in the eighteenth century and changed a world wide enthusiasm into a prosperous sect. This is not true. The seed of the Quakers was sown as widely, if less deeply, than the mental habits of the Puritans. The Quakers, while their energy lasted, permeated every corner of the infant country. . . . Indeed, one need not fear overstatement in saying that the fundamental qualities of what can properly be called the American brand of idealism are essentially Quaker in character and largely Quaker in origin.
>
> ("Quakers and Puritans," *Sat. Rev. of Lit.*, Jan 2, 1926, 457-9)

The means by which a religious movement extends its membership determine to a large degree the nature of the movement. If a religion is propagated by sermons and evangelistic appeals it will tend to rely on words in its worship and it will have recourse to verbal formulae, even though it may have begun with different tendencies and principles. If it is propagated by lectures, discussions, books, and pedagogic methods, it will tend to be intellectual. If it depends on the appeal of ritual, it will become liturgical, however clearly it may be aware of the emptiness of symbols when they become outworn or dissociated from that which they symbolize. We are here reminding ourselves of the fact, well-known but often overlooked, that the means determine the end.

From the outset of the Quaker movement in the middle of the seventeenth century, meetings for worship were based on silence, a silence frequently, but by no means always, broken by spoken words. For this statement we have ample evidence in early Quaker literature. How can such a religion be propagated? Yet propagated it was with power and success, despite extreme persecution by Church and State. How can a religion based primarily on an attempt to heed the voice of God within the soul be communicated to others by outward means? We are thinking not only of its communication to the public, but also to the oncoming generation of its own members.

The claim has frequently been made that early Quakerism spread through evangelism, meaning by that term, fervent preaching to large gatherings. Some Quakers today look back on the beginning as a time when powerful orators converted thousands by their eloquence. These people are saddened because we have no such preachers today. Quaker historians, like all historians, are tempted to emphasize the dramatic for, quite properly, they must make their books interesting if they are to be read. There was much that was highly dramatic in the early years of the Quaker movement. So-called "public Friends" addressed crowds of eager hearers in London, Bristol, and elsewhere. There was preaching along the streets, in market places, and in orchards.

There were also frequent attempts to speak during regular church services after the minister had finished, a practice generally allowed during the Commonwealth period. Sometimes Quakers attempted to speak even before the minister had finished. This was not tolerated. These public appearances often resulted in physical abuse and imprisonment.

Dramatic circumstances were also associated with the incredibly stubborn but passive resistance to persecution: whipping, stoning, fines, imprisonment, banishment. There are no more striking examples of civil disobedience to laws which could not be conscientiously obeyed.

But a careful scrutiny of early Quakerism shows that spectacular events did not constitute the heart and core of the movement. Its real strength lay in the quiet, inconspicuous growth of small meetings in many homes where sometimes as few as three or four waited upon God in silence until one of those present felt moved to speak. Often there was no speaking at all. These small home meetings constituted the seed-bed out of which the Quaker movement grew. This being true, the proclaiming of the message to great crowds was not, and could not have been, the primary factor in the early growth of Quakerism. It was necessary, then as now, that means be consistent with end.

Thus, the method of propagating the faith most often used by the early Friends is not as different from what is possible today as is sometimes supposed. This same method has produced most of the two hundred or more new meetings in America—and others in Europe and Asia—during the last half-century, meetings which have preserved the type of worship characteristic of early Quakerism. The "type," one must say, but not always the same degree of depth and solemnity.

Fortunately we have ample material on why and how people became Friends in the 17th century. This material includes a collection of eye-witness accounts of the beginning of nearly every meeting in England, issued under the title *The First Publishers of Truth* (London: Friends' Historical Society, 1907). Besides these, the Journals tell a great deal about the part that Meeting for Worship plays in the acceptance of the Light as well as in the early struggles for enlightenment.

That the early Quaker Meetings for Worship always began with a period of silence, sometimes a long period, is evident. George Whitehead (1636-1722), who might be called the leading Friend after the death of George Fox, began his travels in the ministry in 1652 at the age of sixteen. He writes in his Journal:

> After some time that I was conversant among our Friends, and frequented the meetings to which I belonged, both in Westmoreland and Yorkshire . . . chiefly between the years of 1652 and 1654, being much inwardly exercised in waiting upon the Lord among them, where we had little preaching, but our meetings kept much and often in Silence, or but few words declared, the Lord was pleased sometimes by his Power and Word of Life, both to tender and open my heart and understanding, so that he gave me (among some others) now and then a few words livingly to utter.
>
> . . .
>
> It was out of these, and such our frequently silent meetings, the Lord was pleased to raise up and bring forth living witnesses, faithful ministers and true prophets. . . . Oh! thus keeping silence before the Lord and thus drawing near to him in a true silent frame of Spirit, to hear first what the Lord speaks to us, before we speak to others.
>
> (*Jour.*, 1725, pp. 10, 11)

George Whitehead's long Journal is filled with accounts of his struggles with government on behalf of persecuted Quakers (he appealed to six successive rulers of England), yet his extraordinary activity was inspired by what he received in the Meeting for Worship.

It is true that some Friends were genuine orators and could address large assemblies with great power, but we find among them too a dependence on the small silent meeting. Edward Burrough (1634-1662), a powerful speaker who was called "Son of Thunder and Consolation," writes in 1658 what was probably the first attempt to give an historical account of the rise of the Quaker movement:

> We met together often, and waited upon the Lord in pure silence, from our own words, and all men's words, and hearkened to the word of the Lord, and felt his word in our hearts. . . . And while waiting upon the Lord in silence, as often we did for many hours together, with our minds and hearts toward him, being stayed in the Light of Christ within us, from all thoughts, fleshly motions, and desires, in our diligent waiting and fear of his name, and hearkening to his Word, we received often the pouring down of the Spirit upon us, and the gift of God's holy, eternal Spirit, as in the days of old, and our hearts were made glad and our tongues loosed, and our mouths opened, and we spake with new tongues as the Lord gave us utterance, and as his Spirit led us.
>
> (*Works of George Fox*. Philadelphia: Gould, 1831, III:13)

Here we have a powerful orator who died in prison, rating his own impressive gift as of secondary importance. His companion, Francis Howgill (1618-1668), who also died in prison, was another speaker who addressed great crowds in London. He writes in his *Testimony concerning Edward Burrough*,

> The Lord of Heaven and Earth we found to be near at hand; and as we waited upon him in pure silence, our minds out of all things, his Dreadful Power, and Glorious Majesty, and Heavenly Presence appeared in our assemblies, when there was no language, tongue or speech from any creature, and the Kingdom of Heaven did gather us, and catch us all, as in a net; and His heavenly Power at one time drew many hundreds to land.
>
> (1662, p. 4)

From this it would appear that the "many hundreds" were drawn more by the numinous power of the silence than by speech.

Such statements as these written by the two greatest speakers at the so-called "threshing meetings" in London would indicate that these meetings were not what have been called revival meetings. This is confirmed in letters written to George Fox by Anthony Pearson (1628-1707) in 1654. He says of the people of London:

> . . . to speak to that in their consciences, to the raising up of the witness, to let them see themselves; and . . . to keep them under from disputing and questioning. This we found the most profitable ministry; and few words must be used; for they have (held) the truth in notions; and all cry out, "What do these men say more than others have said"; but to bring them to silence confounds their wisdom.
>
> (*Letters, etc., of Early Friends,* edited by John Barclay.
> London: Harvey and Darton, 1841, p. 13)

John Burnyeat (1631-1690), convinced in 1653, writes of the early Quaker meetings:

> How were our hearts melted as wax, and our souls poured out as water before the Lord, and our spirits as oil, frankincense and myrrh, offered up unto the Lord as sweet incense, when not a word outwardly in all our assembly had been uttered!
>
> . . . we met together and waited together in silence; it may be sometimes not a word in our meetings for months; but everyone that was faithful waited upon the living word in our own hearts. . . .
>
> (*Jour.,* 1839 ed., p. 159)

Luke Howard (1772-1864), a shoemaker, father of the Dover meeting, and an early convert, writes:

> I may acquaint you a little how things were with us in our first convincement and meetings, after we came to sit down and wait upon the Lord in silence; which was our practice for some years, except when some travelling Friends came amongst us. I can truly say that the Lord was our teacher and his presence and power were manifested amongst us when no words have been sounded in our outward ears.
>
> (*Jour.,* 1707, p. 29)

In the middle of the 17th century, England was swarming with a multitude of small sects. John Gratton (1641-1711) devotes about half of his Journal to his search for a religion which would satisfy him. After trying the Muggletonians and others, he came to a Quaker meeting:

> There was little said in that meeting, but I sat still in it, and was bowed in spirit before the Lord, and felt him with me, and with Friends, and saw they had their minds retired, and waited to feel his presence and power to operate in their hearts, and that they were spiritual worshippers, who worship God in spirit and truth; and I was sensible, that they felt and tasted of the Lord's goodness, as at that time I did; and though few words were spoken, yet I was well satisfied with the meeting, and the presence of the Lord was in the midst of us, and more true comfort, refreshment, and satisfaction did I meet with from the Lord, in that meeting, than ever I had in any meeting in all my life before.
>
> (*Jour.*, 1805, pp. 86-87)

His adherence to the Quaker movement was marked by poetical writing like that of prophets in the Old Testament. A portion of his poem in free verse follows:

> Now, blessed and for ever praised be the Lord God Almighty!
> He hath made glad my soul, and satisfied the breathings of my spirit;
> he hath opened to me the mysteries of his kingdom, and given me a measure of his grace,
> and caused his light to arise in me, and the darkness to flee away;
> he hath given to me the true bread of life, and made my heart glad with the wine of his kingdom:
> he is become my teacher himself, and hath gathered me into his arm of power, and covered me with the banner of his love;
> . . . .
> he hath taken my fetters off from my legs, and hath set my feet upon a sure foundation;
> he hath brought me out of the prison house, and hath set my soul in pleasant places.
>
> (*Jour.*, 1805, p. 91)

The book called *The First Publishers of Truth* names hundreds of men and women often not mentioned in Quaker histories, who gathered in little groups together "to wait upon the Lord in silence" even though "there was none to speak words."

(First Publishers of Truth, ed. 1907, p. 63)

Three quotations from more recent Journals indicate that the strength of Quakerism is still at the motionless center of the wheel. William Hubben (b. 1895) was converted to Quakerism by attending a meeting in Essen, Germany, during the Quaker child-feeding after the first World War.

> Silence, at first, was less gripping and prophetic than I had expected; it had something provocative and trying about it. Only after repeated attendance did this mode of worship appeal to my desire to find a divine-human harmony, producing the assurance of God's presence and removing doubts. And what more could the "Voice of God" be than assurance and the courage to venture forward trusting in His guidance?
>
> *(Jour.*, 1943, p. 213)

Elbert Russell, (1871-1951) relates in his Journal:

> On this particular Wednesday evening there was nothing unusual. It was hot and sultry. The kerosene lamps were dim in the south or men's meeting room. There were not more than a dozen present, men and women about equally divided. These meetings were largely silent. I do not recall any preacher present or spoken message. "Sammy" Spray very often prayed at these meetings and invariably ended his prayer with the words, "Throughout the ceaseless ages of a never-ending eternity." I always hoped he would add "forever" and make it complete.
>
> On this evening a sense of the seriousness of life came to me, and under it I reviewed my conduct and found it unsatisfactory. I saw that the ideals our group of young people were following were unworthy; I had no emotional conviction of sin; but I resolved to turn over a new leaf and occupy myself with worthier things. It marked a stage in my growing up. I tried to behave like a young man and gave up acting like a child. As I look back on this experience, it seems strange to me that there was in it no deep sense of God's presence nor reproaches of conscience. I just put away what had suddenly been revealed to me as wrong.
>
> *(Jour.*, 1956, pp. 34-5)

Alfred Garrett (1867-1946) writes in his Journal:

> While sitting in our Friends' Meeting for Worship in German-

town, there seemed to come out of the silence a quite new and distinct realization of the love of God. I remember considering whether this meant that he loved me or that I loved him: I felt that I had loved him a good deal in the past, but here was something new, something better, stronger, fresher; in fact, that at that very moment God was really loving me. I can now see that this was quite fundamental, if God was really making himself known to me as Love. In fact, might this not be interpreted as a beginning of "revelation"—a mystical perception of the Divine? Many years after, I began to call experiences of this sort, "the discovery of the Divine Love," and to regard them as the most important thing that could befall a human being.

(Jour., 1945, pp. 4-5)

Caroline Stephen (1834-1909) was a member of a famous English literary family. She did not write a Journal, but this quotation from the introduction to her book *Quaker Strongholds* (London: Kegan Paul, Trench, Trubner & Co., Ltd., 1890), is autobiographical.

When lo, on one never-to-be-forgotten Sunday morning, I found myself one of a small company of silent worshipers, who were content to sit down together without words, that each one might feel after and draw near to the Divine Presence, unhindered at least, if not helped, by any human utterance. Utterance I knew was free, should the words be given; and before the meeting was over, a sentence or two were uttered in great simplicity by an old and apparently untaught man, rising in his place amongst the rest of us. I did not pay much attention to the words he spoke, and I have no recollection of their purport. My whole soul was filled with the unutterable peace of the undisturbed opportunity for communion with God, with the sense that at last I had found a place where I might, without the faintest suspicion of insincerity, join with others in simply seeking His presence. To sit down in silence could at the least pledge me to nothing; it might open to me (as it did that morning) the very gate of heaven. And since that day, now more than seventeen years ago, Friends' meetings have indeed been to me the greatest of outward helps to a fuller and fuller entrance into the spirit from which they have sprung; the place of the most soul-subduing, faith-restoring, strengthening, and peaceful communion, in feeding upon the bread of life, that I have ever known. I cannot but believe that what has helped me so unspeakably might be helpful to multitudes in this day of shaking of all that can be shaken, and of restless inquiry after spiritual good. It is in the hope of making more widely known the true source and nature of such spiritual help that I am about to attempt to describe what I have called our strongholds—those principles which cannot fail, whatever may be the future of the Society which for more than two hundred years has taken its stand upon them. I wish to trace, as far as my experience as a "convinced Friend" enables me to do so, what is the true life and strength of our Society; and the manner in which its principles, as actually embodied in its practice, its organization, and, above all, its manner of worship, are fitted to meet the special needs of an important class in our own day.

(pp. 4-5)

So many Quakers in London and Philadelphia have left the Society of Friends to join the Anglican Church, it is interesting to note that Caroline Stephen moved in the opposite direction.

CHAPTER VI

The Spoken Ministry

THE CHANGES which I have described as taking place within the Quaker Journalists are not always noticeable to their families or friends. Sooner or later it becomes necessary for each of them to take a public stand. Some action is required. Action also enables the Journalist to become more established in a new way of life. Inward change is not enough by itself to "clinch the nail."

There are two actions which enable families and friends to discover what has happened—often much to their surprise. These two public stands are: entrance on the vocal ministry and the adoption of "plain" speech, "plain" dress, and "plain" behavior. Once the Journalist has publicly taken either or both of these actions, he or she will then feel compelled to live consistently with that action. In general such a stand requires a faithful endeavor to live up to what is required by Christ in the Gospels.

This does not mean that this requirement can be fully met. The writer will often feel that the high standard of behavior has not been attained. Nevertheless, perfection in attainment requires only that the measure of Light which has been given, however limited, has been followed. The measure may be small compared to the perfection at which the writer aims. But if the writer is faithful to the measure of Light which is given, inward peace is secured and anxiety disappears—a situation very different from that which appears in the Puritan journals. The Quaker writer almost always describes a sense of complete inward peace whenever a difficult requirement of the Light has been met.

In most cases the inward concern requiring public expression in meeting is faced with much hesitancy. Speaking in meeting may be postponed, sometimes for many years. This hesitancy results in great inward anxiety until the writer possesses enough courage to stand up in meeting and face family and friends, often surprising them by a performance which they did not expect. (The average age on entering the ministry of 100 Journalists examined by the present writer comes to about 26 years.)

The first vocal expression in meeting is often preceded by what is considered to be frivolous behavior and a lack of seriousness. This behavior makes the first appearance in the ministry especially difficult, since family and friends are so surprised at the change from a frivolous child to a serious minister of the gospel. Generally when the very difficult decision has been made to become a "public Friend," the life of a writer is, from then on, quite different. Friends and relatives expect him to live up to his new role.

In the early days of the Society the intense enthusiasm generated by an exciting new discovery in religion led many into the ministry as soon as they joined the movement. But sometimes in the early days, and as a rule in the later days, the ministry was entered only after a long struggle. Charles Marshall (1637-1698), one of the most fearless of the early Friends, writes:

> So hard was it for me to open my mouth in those meetings at Bristol that had not the Lord caused his power to be manifest in my heart as new wine in a vessel that wanted vent, I might have perished.
>
> (*Jour.*, F. L. IV:130)

"My natural disposition," writes Thomas Arnett, "had a great aversion to becoming a mouth for the Almighty." (*Jour.*, 1884, p. 20)

John Yeardley (1786-1858) thus records his resistance: "Went to meeting this morning with a painful apprehension lest I should expose myself in that which is so contrary to my natural inclination." (*Jour.*, 1860, p. 35). After eleven years of struggle he writes:

> I felt myself in such a resigned state of mind in our little week-day meeting that I could not doubt the time was fully come for

me to be relieved from that state of unspeakable oppression which my poor mind had been held in for so many years past.

(*Ibid.*, p. 28)

John Churchman was surprised to find that he could decide to speak without difficulty. After eight years of hesitation, he records:

As I sat in a week day meeting, I had a few words fresh before me, with a gentle motion to deliver them, which I feared to omit, still remembering what followed a former neglect, so I expressed what was on my mind, and therein had peace.

(*Jour.*, 1779, p. 24)

Martha Routh (1743-1817) felt called to the ministry at fourteen, but after a long and severe conflict which nearly resulted in her death, and during which her large school diminished to three pupils, her "bonds were broken" at the age of twenty-nine. "After resignation took place," she writes, "I scarcely knew how I was raised from my seat to say: 'Keep thy foot, when thou goest into the house of the Lord; and be more willing to hear, than to offer the sacrifice of fools.'" (*Jour.*, 1822, p. 31) This sermon succeeded in silencing a "ranting" speaker. Later Martha Routh was to travel on horseback thousands of miles in the ministry throughout the American colonies.

Hugh Judge (1750-1834) worked in a mill on the Wissahickon. What follows is his account of his beginning in the vocal ministry:

. . . when we got into town, being in Second street, I found Friends were going to evening meeting; which I had not thought of till then. So I concluded I would also go to the meeting, and did so; but had not the least thought of having anything to say, till the meeting was gathered. Then I felt the power of God to be upon me in such a manner as I had never felt it before. I trembled exceedingly, though I strove against it; but all to no purpose. Now was the time of proving—now the full time was come. I thought if I had been at a little meeting in the country, it would not have been so hard to deliver what appeared to be my duty at that time, which was on this wise: Obedience is required of thee, O man—obedience to the law of thy God. This arose with great clearness, and some more which I do not dis-

tinctly remember. But alas! for me: I could not think of speaking
in so great a gathering of people; and then it occurred to my
mind that I was not a proper member. So that I did absolutely
refuse, and was going to get up and go out of the meeting; but
I durst not, there was such a great dread over me. I therefore kept
my seat; though I could see no way to have peace but by expressing what was on my mind, and this was like death to me at that
time. Through my strugglings and strivings against it, I was thrown
into great disorder and distress of mind. Horror and darkness
came over me, accompanied with this language: The fountain
shall be sealed, and thou shall draw no more living waters there-
from. This was spoken as clear and as plain to my spiritual senses,
as it could have been to my outward ear; and it was alarming to
me. I had not met with anything more awakening. I then, and
not before, gave up, and resigned all up, saying, Here am I, Lord,
do with me what thou pleasest. Give me strength, I pray thee,
to do the thing thou requirest of me. My will being thus given
up, I felt the returns of his presence and power, and with great
clearness and an audible voice, I delivered what was before me,
as already mentioned. But Oh! my pen is not able to set forth the
awful solemn quiet,—the calm, serene, sweet state of mind that I
enjoyed for many days: so that it seemed as if I had got into
another world.

(Jour., 1841, pp. 8-10)

John Comly felt at fifteen that he could become a minister,
but he did not preach until he was twenty-nine. Mary Alexander
(1760-1810) received her first intimation at seventeen. At twenty-
nine, "A light shone round my bed and I heard a voice intel-
ligibly say 'Thou art appointed to preach the gospel.'" (Jour.,
1811, p. 20) This ended her conflict. John J. Cornell (1826-
1909) at nineteen heard a voice which said, "I shall call thee
into the work of the ministry," (Jour., 1906, p. 23) but he did
not preach until he was thirty. Joseph Hoag (1762-1853) received the call at the age of twelve and spoke at twenty, after
"the Lord said to my spiritual ear, 'Take thy choice decidedly
for thou shalt have no longer time to be waited upon.'" (Jour.,
1860, p. 45)

Isaac Martin (1758-1828) of Rahway, New Jersey began his
extensive ministry at the age of thirty.

I felt a concern to stand up, with a few words; but fearing lest I should be deceived, I earnestly besought the Lord for preservation from going too fast. . . . I had learned a good degree of resignation to the Lord's requirings; and my will being now in subjection, He was pleased to furnish me with a clear evidence of my duty. . . . Although I did not feel a very extraordinary degree of life and power, whilst speaking, nor yet such precious incomes of love and peace after sitting down, as some I have read of (which occasioned some exercise to my mind), . . . I desired to be content; . . . The sweet refreshment intended for me was withheld about two days, when my heart was unusually tendered and contrited before the Lord.

(*Jour.*, 1834, pp. 15-16)

Although he was always in ill health, possibly a result of mercury poisoning since he was a hatter by trade, Isaac Martin's Journal is a record of almost continual travels in the ministry.

Rufus Hall (1744-1805) was worried:

One thing often came into my mind, that seemed to be a mystery—it was this: how a minister of the gospel knew that he was rightly called to that weighty work; or how did he know when to stand up and what to say?

(*Jour.*, 1840, pp. 7, 11-12)

He found out when, in a dream, he spoke so loudly that he woke himself up.

Few like Allen Jay (1831-1910) were made hesitant by an impediment in speech, though John Richardson (1666-1753) was cured of stammering by speaking in meeting. James Gough (1712-1780) was so embarrassed when he first spoke that he held his hat before his eyes, but he writes that after he sat down, "a flood of divine joy poured into my heart." (*Jour.*, 1783, p. 39)

Occasionally the inner conflict over the hesitancy to speak in meeting appears in dreams. Dr. John Rutty of Dublin enters in his diary, "A dream that I shall receive a call to the ministry: but Satan buffets: Lord rebuke him." (*Jour.*, 1796, p. 101) A striking example of this conflict, as far as its expression in dreams is concerned, is that of David Ferris, who resisted the call for fifteen years. He records three dreams which represent his inner conflict. One of these dreams is as follows:

One night I dreamed that I saw a large, spacious building, in an unfinished state; and the master builder, who appeared an excellent person, came to me as I stood at a distance, and desired me to go and take a view of it; to which I agreed; and as we were surveying it and examining the particular parts I observed that among the many pillars, erected for the support of the building, there was one lacking. I queried of him, what was the cause of that vacancy. He replied, it was left for me; and that I was specially designed and prepared for the place, and showed me how I fitted it, like a mortise is fitted to its tenon. So that I saw in my dream that all he said was true. But, notwithstanding all this, I objected to my capacity and fitness to fill the vacancy, and was therefore unwilling to occupy it. He endeavored, by the most convincing reasons, to remove all my objections, and to demonstrate that I was fitted for the place. He further told me that they had not another prepared for it; and that the building would be retarded if I did not comply with the design. After he had reasoned with me a long time, and I still refused, he appeared to be grieved, and told me it was a great pity that I should be rendered useless in the house by my own obstinacy; and then added, "But it must not be so; for if thou wilt not be a pillar, thou shalt be a plank for the floor." He then showed me how I might be flattened and prepared for that purpose. But I refused that place also, on the ground that it looked too diminutive to be a plank to be trod upon by all that came into the house.

(Jour., 1855, pp. 61-2)

In traveling with Comfort Hoag, David was twice asked by her, "Why did thee not speak?" Finally she prayed, in secret, that her life might be taken if David did not speak. This got him on his feet. *(Ibid.,* p. 68)

Samuel Bownas (1676-1753) was "reached" by a sermon aimed directly at him.

One first-day, being at meeting, a young woman named Anne Wilson was there and preached; she was very zealous, and fixing my eye upon her, she, with a great zeal, pointed her finger at me, uttering these words with much power, "A traditional Quaker, thou comest to meeting as thou went from it the last time, and goest from it as thou came to it, but art no better for thy coming, what wilt thou do in the end?" This was so pat to my then condition, that, like Saul, I was smitten to the ground, as it might be said, but turning my thoughts inward, in secret I cried, *Lord, what shall I do to help it?* And a voice as it were spoke in my heart, saying, *Look unto me, and I will help thee.* . . . I went home with a heavy heart, and could neither eat nor sleep as I used to do, but my work never succeeded better in my hands than it did at this time, nor my mind never less in it. . . . I longed for the meeting day, and thought it a very long week. When the time of meeting came, my mind was soon fixed and staid upon God, and I found an uncommon enjoyment that gave me great satisfaction. . . . I began to see and understand the Scriptures, and the nature of preaching the doctrine of the gospel in the power and spirit, plainly seeing a difference between a preacher of the letter and of the spirit, which till then I was wholly ignorant of.

(*Jour.*, 1805, pp. 14-15)

Eventually meetings appointed elders to advise the ministers, and the elders generally made a special effort to see to it that a minister lived up to his words. Members of the immediate family of a new speaker were expected, also, to act as consistent Friends. Another function of the elders is to encourage or discourage ministers. In some cases silent potential ministers have been given encouragement to speak.

In his Journal John Rutty asks: "Lord, if I be not a knife among the utensils of the spiritual house, make me a whetstone!" (*Jour.*, 1796, p. 242) A whetstone could be compared to the function of an elder and a knife to that of a minister.

Since no minister feels personally responsible for what is said in meeting, words of praise or blame should be given very carefully. Jesse Kersey (1768-1846), a potter of Chester County, is reputed to have been the most eloquent minister of his time. He was concerned that the "sincere-hearted (be) encouraged, and the self-sufficient warned."

When an instrument has been qualified to deliver a powerful and baptizing testimony, there are sometimes found those who extol him and thereby endanger his standing by raising in him a High opinion of his own qualifications. This applause of the instrument is always improper, and if the minister is not well guarded, may produce a very dangerous opinion of his own consequence.

(*Jour.*, 1851, p. 166)

Nearly all Quakers who became ministers traveled from one meeting to another after securing a minute from their monthly meetings which endorsed their ministry. This gave them the power to call special meetings and not wait until First Day meeting in order to speak. This practice did much to hold the Society together. Almost all Friends who became ministers followed a "concern" of their own to travel.

Since Friends in the ministry only speak when inspired to speak, it happens sometimes that there is no speech because there is no inspiration. A traveling Friend might find that announcements of his coming have been sent to the whole neighborhood, the meeting house is filled, and he has nothing to say. Job Scott reports:

> I had sat through eleven meetings in silence one after another, except a very few words just at the close of the first of them. Now, in all these silent meetings I could never once, except those few words, find ability or openness to say a single word, and believe my silence was wholly ordered of God, though contrary to the desires of many.
>
> (*Jour.*, 1831, p. 207)

In the Journals the writer never says "I preached" or "I spoke in meeting." Rather such expressions are used as "the power of the Lord rose up" or "the presence of the Spirit was felt in the meeting." John Churchman uses the following expressions:

"I had close work."
"I stood up with a large opening."
"I had a draft that way."
"Truth favored to a degree of openness."
"Owned by Truth."

At a time when he was a member of a group visiting families, Churchman omitted to say to one family what was on his mind. After he had returned home alone, he felt so uncomfortable because of this omission, that he went back to express his concern. At the end of the return journey, he could say, "I enjoyed great peace." (*Jour.*, 1779, p. 21)

Some Friends became ministers while acting as traveling companions to ministers. Christine Majolier Alsop (1805-1879) found it an easy transition from interpreting for Friends' ministers to interpreting for the Lord.

Catherine Phillips had just such traveling ministers as Comfort Hoag and Anne Wilson in mind when she wrote:

> Here I suggest some cautions necessary to be observed by young women in a single state, who travel in the service of the ministry, towards those of the other sex, who are also unmarried.
>
> First, to guard their own minds, lest they admit of any pleasing imagination, and stamp it with the awful name of revelation; and so slide into a familiarity and freedom of conversation and behaviour, which might tend to engage the affections of young men. Secondly, to endeavor to retain a feeling sense of the state of the spirits of those with whom they are intimate, and strictly to observe their conduct and behaviour towards them: so will they be the better able to judge of their motives for accompanying them, or of any other act of kindness; and may wisely check any forward thought which looks beyond friendship which may easily be done by some prudent remarks (yet obliquely) in conversation. Thirdly, to beware of hurting any of these tender plants by an austere conduct. When we are singularly made instruments of good, in the hand of Providence, to any soul, there is a natural aptitude to lean a little to the instrument, and to prefer it above others, which for a time may be allowable. The Lord, leading the mind by gradual steps from the love of other objects to the entire love of himself . . . may permit it for a season to lean to an instrument in which case a prudent reserve is necessary, as well as a tender regard to the growth of the party thus visited. I confess it is sometimes a nice point, to be ready to be of service to such, and preserve the unity of the spirit, free from mixture of natural affection; a distinction which I fear has been overlooked by some to their great hurt.
>
> (*Jour.*, 1798, pp. 111-12)

Some ministers, like Churchman, began their careers in the vocal ministry during family visits. A notable family visitor was Elizabeth Newport (1796-1872). In a memoir compiled by Ann Townsend, there are records of visits to as many as ten families a day.

> We visited seven families that day and seven yesterday, although it stormed hard. Today E. has been very poorly, indeed the ex-

ercise of her mind is so great that her physical powers seem scarcely able at times to support her. Those sitting quietly at home can form no idea of the travail of spirit it requires for this family visiting.

(Jour., 1878, p. 62)

At these visits, Elizabeth Newport frequently exhibited what can be properly called clairvoyance, in which she was able to discern the future or to reveal conditions within a person not known to any but themselves.

In another instance, where there was a large family of sons and daughters, Elizabeth addressed them with a power that had a tendency to bring conviction with it. She then particularized one son upon whom she felt that the anointing oil had been poured, and that if faithful to his calling he would have to invite others to enter the Lord's vineyard and labor in His cause. To one of the daughters she spoke, tenderly alluding to what she believed she would have to pass through. That it would be her privilege to nurse her beloved father, who would ere long be taken ill— that by her devoted care, the pain which he would have to endure would be in a degree assuaged; and after all had been done, and his loved form committed to the dust, in a brief space she would follow him to the mansions of bliss. Trying as this was to some of the family at the time to hear, it proved a true prophecy. Within a few months the father and daughter were taken hence, and in not a very long time, the son alluded to, was acknowledged as a Gospel minister.

(Ibid., pp. 48-9)

With other Friends, Elizabeth Newport visited President Pierce. The story of this visit occupies more than five pages of her memoir and so is too long to quote. She comforted the President who had recently lost his only son. She called him "brother" and he called her "sister." Their words to each other were eloquent and affecting, especially on the subjects of war and slavery. The President was evidently much moved by this visit *(Ibid.,* pp. 155-60).

Experiences which might be called telepathic were not unusual with Quaker traveling ministers. John William Graham, in an address to the Friends' Historical Society, reports a number of divine leadings with no apparent human agency. (Graham. *Psychical Experiences of Quaker Ministers*. London: Friends' Historical Society, 1933). "These telepathic phenomena . . . are plainly connected with the rest of the ministerial endowment of the seers, and that endowment is a function of the keen and pervasive spiritual life, peculiar among men, and carried out as part of the service of that remarkable institution, the traveling ministry of the Society of Friends." (p. 2)

One of the most extraordinary instances is that involving James Dickinson and Jane Fearon. (The details of the story appear in volume five, pages 181-187 of the Friends' Miscellany, 1833. No mention of it is to be found in Dickinson's Journal in the Friends' Library.) In 1690 the two Friends, traveling together in the ministry, stopped for the night at a lonely house. Jane Fearon felt inexplicably afraid during the evening meal and by the middle of the night they had heard enough ominous talk to make them run away. James Dickinson felt very clearly guided to a place where the nearby river could be forded and to a refuge in which they would not be seen, even by daylight. Pursuers with dogs, came after them but they escaped being found. In the morning, Dickinson felt equally strongly guided to return to the house for their horses and baggage. This proved to be safe. Many weeks later, coming back to that area, they discovered that the house had been torn down and a number of bodies discovered of persons who had been murdered and apparently partly eaten. They had been served human flesh to eat on their first visit.

John Richardson tells of a leading he received while traveling in the ministry:

> As we came near a great house in Maryland, I espied a little white horse, the sight of which put me in mind of a dream I had on board the ship before I landed, in which I thought I got a little white horse, which carried me well, and many miles. I said to the Friends with me, Let us call at this house, which we did, and upon inquiry about a horse, the man said he had none but a little white young galloway, as he called it, which he was willing to sell, and told us it carried him one day forty miles. He asked eight pounds sterling for it, and I bade him five pounds sterling;

the man's wife coming up the passage heard what I had offered, and she said to her husband, It is enough, so I had him, and a good horse he proved, and carried me, by a moderate computation, four thousand miles.

(Jour., 1856, p. 54)

Such experiences may occur among Quaker traveling ministers because of the nature of the Quaker meeting for worship. Friends do not engage in intellectual reasoning or in recalling the past. Their primary object is to increase as much as possible their inward sensitivity and awareness. A story from Alfred Garrett's biography of Stephen Grellet *(Quaker Biographies.* Philadelphia: 1910, IV:130-256) is worth retelling. "There is an incident related of Stephen Grellet, which though the time of its occurrence does not seem to be remembered, may properly be recorded here." (p. 155). Stephen Grellet, on his way to preach in a lumber camp while in America, came to a deserted camp and felt impelled to preach in one of the empty huts, though nobody was in sight. He then returned without going further. Years later a man stopped him as he was crossing London Bridge, saying that, returning to the old camp for some forgotten tools, he had heard the sermon, been changed by it, and that as a result of this not less than a thousand souls had been saved.

Isaac Sharpless (1848-1920), who was for many years President of Haverford College, wrote an autobiographical book entitled *The Quaker Boy on the Farm and at School* in which he describes the Quaker Meeting which he attended while a student at Westtown School. One meeting especially, attended by sixty members of the Westtown School Committee, was made up of the most weighty Friends of the Philadelphia Yearly Meeting.

> The broad-brimmed hats of the men surmounting the smooth-shaven face and long, straight-collared coat, the ponderous bonnets of the women, including a quiet face encased in an immaculate cap, with a "handkerchief" around the shoulders of the same ephemeral material, made an impression of saintliness not forgotten. . . .
>
> The Spirit of youth was awed and he heard, as from an oracle, the prayer or the preaching which presently was sounded, as if it were the voice of God, as indeed it sometimes was. It was seldom emotional. Its burden was to induce the hearers to yield the heart

to the operations of the Heavenly Guide, and thereby grow in grace. These Divine visitations would become more frequent and definite and potential as the result of obedience. The impulses to good were to be found within, rather than without, and would become rules of life, as well as spiritual influences.

(*Jour.*, Philadelphia: The Biddle Press, 1908, pp. 37, 38)*

---

* It should be noted that today it is no longer the practice in the Society of Friends to designate certain persons in the meeting as "approved ministers." The ministry now is more widely shared by persons in all parts of the congregations and is no longer confined largely to the facing bench. As a result there is much less traveling in the ministry than formerly. The ministry has become more secular in character and deals with social problems more than religious problems in the narrower sense of the word religious. There is accordingly less solemnity, awe, and reverence, but more concern with problems of everyday life. This fits in with the Quaker doctrine that all life is sacramental, however unimportant any event related in the meeting might seem. Traveling in the ministry today is more likely to occur as a result of an invitation to a speaker to give a lecture outside of the meeting for worship than as a self-assumed concern.

CHAPTER VII

Adoption of Plain Speech, Plain Dress, and Simple Living

WE have already pointed out the most important way in which the Quaker Journalist might inform his family and friends that he had become what is sometimes called a "public Friend." The second way might precede or it might accompany his entrance into the ministry. Adoption of what is called "plainness" in speech, dress, and behavior was a notice to the world of what he stood for. The adoption of this so-called "plainness" also served to encourage the Quaker to live up to his principles.

The word "plain" had a special meaning. It did not just mean simplicity. The word "sincerity" would be more accurate. Plainness involved the determination to treat all other persons as equals. In England in the 17th and 18th centuries there were very definite differences between classes in society. Some words were used only to persons in a higher class and other words were used to members of a lower class. The Quakers would not use words which designated class distinctions. Thus they would not follow the custom of saying "you" to a superior and "thou" or "thee" to an inferior, but they would use "thou" and "thee" to all persons including royalty, judges, and parents.

William Edmundson (1627-1712) was traveling in the ministry when he came to the town of Finagh in Ireland, where he had to stay overnight in an ale-house run by the constable.

> I alighted, went into the House, and there were Troopers drinking, who soon perceived what I was, and began to scoff and

to ask me many Questions, which I answered in my Freedom; but when I Thee'd and Thou'd them in our Discourse, they were very angry, and one of them swore *If I Thou'd him again, he would cleave my Head;* but in our Discourse, when it came in its Place I Thou'd him again, and he starting up in Anger drew his Sword; but one of his Corporals sitting by him stopped him, and commanded him to put up his Sword, for there should be no Cleaving of Heads there.

(Jour., 1774, p. 31)

There were at least three reasons why Quakers would not say "Your Honor" to an official: first, it might not be true; second, it designated a class distinction; and third, it was a form of flattery. The same is true of many other words used in addressing others: "your humble servant," "Mr. and Mrs." (i.e. "Master and Mistress"), "your majesty," "your grace," etc. George Fox records in his Journal:

"Why," says he, "when Major Ceely and I came by you when you were walking in the Castle Green, he doffed his hat to you and said 'How do you, Mr. Fox? Your servant, Sir.' Then you said unto him, 'Major Ceely, take heed of hypocrisy and a rotten heart, for when came I to be thy master and thee my servant?"

(Jour., 1952 ed., p. 250)

When a Quaker becomes a minister and travels in the ministry, or when he adopts the peculiarities of Quaker behavior, he is no longer an individual but feels himself to be a member of a community. Thomas Ellwood (1639-1713) records the result of a meeting with some old companions:

When I had set up my Horse, I went directly to the Hall, where the Sessions were held; where I had been but a very little while, before a Knot of my old Acquaintances espying me, came to me. One of these was a Scholar in his gown; another a Surgeon of that City (both my School-Fellows, and Fellow Boarders at *Thame-School;* and the Third a Country Gentleman, with whom I had long been very familiar.)

When they were come up to me, they all saluted me, after the usual manner, putting off their Hats and Bowing; and saying, "Your Humble Servant, Sir," expecting, no doubt, the like from me. But when they saw me stand still, not moving my Cap, nor bowing my Knee in the way of *Congee* to them; they were amazed and looked first one upon another, then upon me, and then upon one another again for a while, without a Word speaking.

At length the Surgeon (a brisk young Man) who stood nearest to me, clapping his Hand, in a familiar way, upon my Shoulder, and smiling on me, said, "What, Tom, a Quaker?" To which I readily and cheerfully Answered, "Yes: a Quaker." And as the Words passed out of my Mouth, I felt Joy spring in my Heart; for I rejoyced, that I had not been drawn out by them, into a Compliance with them; and that I had Strength and Boldness given me, to Confess myself to be one of that despised people.

(Jour., 1714, p. 63)

John Barclay writes as follows after he first speaks in meeting:
. . . what I have desired has often been, the unity of the church and love of the brethren.

(Jour., 1877, p. 208)

Because Quakers felt their oneness with a community so strongly, few of them stand out prominently as individuals. This has tended to lead historians to ignore individuals among them in spite of their wide influence in their own time and their numbers so widely dispersed.

Refusal to put off their hats in deference to others was one of the most noticeable indications of the Quaker determination to treat all other persons as equals. The following incidents from Fox's Journal are typical:

And a great rage there was amongst professors and priests, for they said, "They *thee* and *thou* all people without respect, and will not doff their hats to one nor bow the knee to any man." And this troubled them fearfully. But at the Assizes they expected we should have been all hanged. "And then," said they, "let's see whether they dare *thou* and *thee* and keep on their hats before the judge." But all this was little to us, for we saw how God would stain the world's honour and glory; for we were commanded not to seek that honour nor give it but know the honour that came from God only and seek for that. . . .

And they brought us into the court, where we stood with our hats on a pretty while, and all was quiet.

And I was moved to say: "Peace be amongst you."

And at last Judge Glynne, the Lord Chief Justice of England, a Welshman, said to the gaoler:

"What be these you have brought here into court?"

"Prisoners, my Lord," said he.

"Why do not you put off your hats?" said the judge.

And we said nothing.

Then again the judge:

"The court commands you to put off your hats."

And then I replied and said, "Where did ever any magistrate, king, or judge from Moses to Daniel command any such thing in all their courts or their kings or judges? Or show me where it is written or printed in any law of England where any such thing is commanded; show it me and I will put off my hat."

And then the judge grew very angry and said, "I do not carry my law books on my back."

Then said I, "Tell me where it is printed in a statute book that I may read it."

Then said the judge, "Take him away, prevaricator, I'll firk (i.e. trounce) him."

Then they took us away and put us amongst the thieves; and presently after he calls to the gaoler, "Bring them up again."

"Come," said he, "where had they hats from Moses to Daniel? Come, answer me, I have you fast now," said he.

Then I said, "Thou mayest read in the third of Daniel that the three children were cast into the fiery furnace by Nebuchadnezzar with their cloaks, hose, and hats on. And you may see that Nebuchadnezzar was not offended at their hats."

(Jour., 1952 ed., pp. 242-44)

For some, to whom it was a real sacrifice, the testimony against "hat honor" marked the chief turning point in the conversion process. Joseph John Gurney (1788-1847) records how he lost his high social standing by entering a drawing room with his hat on.

Soon after my return home, I was engaged to a dinner party at the house of one of our first county gentlemen. Three weeks before the time was I engaged, and three weeks was my young mind in agitation, from the apprehension, of which I could not dispossess myself, that I must enter his drawing room with my hat on. From the sacrifice, strange and unaccountable as it may appear, I could not escape. In a Friend's attire, and with my hat on, I entered the drawing room at the dreaded moment, shook hands with the mistress of the house, went back into the hall, deposited my hat, spent a rather comfortable evening, and returned home in some degree of peace. I had afterwards the same thing to do at the Bishop's; the result was, that I found myself the decided Quaker, was perfectly understood to have assumed that character, and to dinner parties, except in the family circle, was asked no more. . . .

I have no wish to repeat what then happened; but I dare not regret a circumstance which was, under the Divine blessing made the means of fully deciding my course, and thus of facilitating my future progress.

(Jour., 1854, I:95-7)

Thomas Ellwood marked the same determination by keeping his hat on in front of his father. (He lost three hats doing this.) He also records this incident:

While I was then in London, I went to a little Meeting of Friends, which was then held in the House of one Humphry Bache, a Goldsmith, at the Sign of the Snail in Tower street. It was then a very troublesome time, not from the Government, but from the Rabble of Boys and rude People, who upon the Turn of the Times (at the return of the King) took liberty to be very abusive.

When the Meeting ended, a pretty Number of these unruly Folk were got together at the Door, ready to receive the Friends as they came forth, not only with evil words, but with Blows; which I saw they bestowed freely on some of them that were gone out before me, and expected I should have my Share of, when I came amongst them. But quite contrary to my Expectation, when I came out, they said one to another, "Let him alone; Don't meddle with him: he is no Quaker, I'll warrant you."

This struck me, and was worse to me, than if they had laid their Fists on me, as they did on others. I was troubled to think what the Matter was, or what these Rude People saw in me that made them not take me for a Quaker. And upon a close Examination of my self, with respect to my Habit and Deportment, I could not find anything to place it on; but that I had then on my Head a large *Mountier-Cap* of Black Velvet, the Skirt of which being turned up in Folds, looked (it seems) somewhat above the then Common Garb of a Quaker; and this put me out of Conceit with my Cap.

(Jour., 1714, pp. 105-6)

The Quaker bonnet, considered the epitome of "plainness" for more than one hundred years, came to America in 1795 on the head of Martha Routh, an English Friend traveling in the ministry.* Her bonnet was of the same pattern as those worn

---

* Gummere, A. M. *The Quaker, A Study in Costume.* 1901, p. 190.

by fashionable ladies in Paris, and later Queen Victoria, except
that it had no ornaments or plumes. Quakers did not trim their
bonnets to suit the changing fashions. After meeting one morning in Philadelphia, Ann Warder, a visitor from England, was
approached by a concerned Friend:

> She had been told of my getting a whalebone bonnet. The idea
> of my being persuaded to alter in dress had much distressed her
> & she begged me to be cautious. I told her I had not the most dis-
> tant view there was any difference in their plainness, provided the
> pattern did not vary. . . . I afterwards determined rather than give
> any one pain, I would save the one which was really made to take
> home, instead of getting another.
>
> (*Jour.*, 1786, I:74-5)

Quaker simplicity did not lie so much in the wearing of peculiar garments as in resisting the changing whims of fashion.
John Comly writes of his first Sunday coat:

> In those early days of which I have been speaking, it was cus-
> tomary for quite small boys to have what would now be called long-
> tailed coats as their first-day dress. On my parents furnishing me
> with an opportunity of having a coat of this description of home-
> made cloth, they gave me the choice of having it made plain,
> or with cross pockets, such as my father always wore. I chose to
> have it made plain; and never had one made otherwise. What-
> ever principle it was that then determined my election, I be-
> lieve it has many times since been a blessing to me, as a monitor
> to remind me of a plainness of conduct corresponding with the cut
> of my coat.
>
> (*Jour.*, 1853, p. 20)

Quaker children who were required to wear so-called plain
dress often suffered because of their peculiar appearance.

> When between eight and ten years of age, my father and mother
> sent me near two miles to school, to *Richard Scorver,* in the sub-
> urbs of *London.* I went mostly by myself to the school; and many
> and various were the exercises I went through, by beatings and
> stonings along the street, being distinguished to the people (by the
> badge of plainness which my parents put upon me) of what pro-
> fession I was; divers telling me, "'Twas no more sin to kill me
> than it was to kill a dog."
>
> (Thomas Chalkley, *Jour.*, 1754, p. 2)

Inazo Nitobe (1862-1933) was convinced of Quakerism while at
Johns Hopkins University. His adherence to the Shinto religion
predisposed him to simplicity, or "purity" as understood by
Shintoism.

> I was particularly edified by the doctrine that each man was a
> light unto himself, and sufficient, too; further, that if he lived up
> to his own light, he could do anything—whatever others might say
> of him. The teaching was reassuring. In a measure I got rid of my
> extreme sensitiveness to the opinion of others.
>
> *(Jour.,* 1934, p. 39)

After he arrived in the United States he attended church now
and then, visiting the Methodist congregations first and then
others, but making no permanent connections. One day as he
strolled along in Baltimore he saw women in plain dress emerg-
ing from the small Friends meeting house. He asked his companion what this unusual costume meant. His friend knew
enough about Quakers to explain, and the next Sunday Inazo
Nitobe attended meeting. During his years of study he had become something of a skeptic, doubtful of the value of a sermon
preached weekly by a man whose duty it was to preach, and he
had reached the position that inspiration should come directly
from the Divine, that man should commune with God without
intermediary. When he came into meeting at Baltimore, he saw
no pulpit, heard no hymns and no ritual, felt the meditative
silence in which the message took its shape, and listened to the
words spoken. He was profoundly moved. He began to attend
regularly and on Twelfth Month 9th, 1886, he was received into
membership by Baltimore Monthly Meeting.

Another aspect of the early Friends' concern for plainness was
their opposition to wearing dyed clothing. They thought that
the dye concealed dirt and injured the cloth. John Woolman
was looked upon by some of his friends with suspicion because
he wore a white hat just when they were coming into fashion.
Joshua Evans (1731-1798) found in himself too great a "sensi-
tiveness to the opinion of others" as he tried to carry out this
concern.

> After wearing my old hat until it began to look too mean, I went
> to Philadelphia intending to get a white one; but returned without

letting my exercise be known, by obtaining it. Not attending to the pointings of the inward monitor, the first time, I had to make another trial: then, again, through weakness, my resolution failed me, and I procured a black hat. This pretty soon brought on me such trouble for my disobedience to Him who waited to be gracious, that I thought I felt the terrors occasioned by guilt both day and night, until I became willing to be accounted a fool, and to confess my fault to the man I got the hat of; which I did, and offered to pay him for the damage done, if he would take it again, and inform me where I could get a white one; which he complied with. My mind was then much humbled, but not low enough yet; for again I returned home without buying a white hat. But I again felt the righteous chastisements of the Lord, under which my supplication was that he might have mercy upon me, a poor weak creature. Then, deeply in the cross, I went to the place I had been informed of, and bought a white hat; with which I returned in the enjoyment of sweet peace of mind. I also procured stockings made of white wool, and wore them, and also my new hat; and so far I felt easy in my mind.

(*Jour.*, 1837, pp. 24-5)

Plainness was sometimes a means of self-discipline by which a person's own will was controlled. When Elizabeth Ashbridge said to little Sarah Stephenson (1738-1802), "What a pity that a child should have a ribbon on her hair," the child felt the "weight of her manner" as well as her "unspeakable love."

Her words were piercing, and deeply affected my mind. I do not know that I closed my eyes to sleep that night; and in the morning, not daring to put on my ribbon, I came down without it. Yet I had many fears, expecting to be censured by one of the family, as having left it off to get the favour of the friends: and from this unjust ground, the enemy caused many seasons of sorrow. This was coming a little to the gate of stripping, which work went gradually forward.

(*Jour.*, 1807, pp. 14-5)

By such "stripping" we are, of course, to understand the removal of any obstacle to the soul's progress, and the chief of those obstacles was pride. Granted that there was sometimes pride in plainness, an examination of the Journals clearly shows that "going plain" marked a real and sometimes supremely important milestone in the Pilgrim's Progress of the Quaker.

One feature of the doctrine of simplicity is omission of the sacraments. Quakers consider these in their physical form, to be superfluous. Samuel Bownas was imprisoned on Long Island in 1703 for speaking "scandalous lies of, and reflections against the Church of England" although the grand jury refused to indict him and the trial jury refused to convict him. (They both brought in the verdict: "Ignoramus.")

I had in this time of confinement sundry visits. . . . The first was by an Indian King, with three of his chief men with him . . . his nation was much wasted and almost extinct, so that he had but a small people to rule. However, there was in him some marks of superiority above the other three who attended him, who shewed some regard to him as their sovereign. . . .

The king asked, *if I was a Christian.* I told him I was. *And are they,* said he, *Christians too that keep you here?* I said they professed themselves to be so. Then he and his company shewed their admiration, that one Christian could do this to another. And then he enquired concerning the difference between me and them. I replied, it consisted of sundry particulars; first my adversaries hold with sprinkling a little water on the face of an infant, using a form of words, and the ceremony of making the sign of a cross with their finger on the babe's forehead, called this baptism, and urging it as essential to future happiness: and I, with my brethren, can see no good in this ceremony.—Here they talked one with another again, but I understood them not. After which they asked me, *If I thought there was nothing in this ceremony of good, to secure our future happiness?* I said, I see nothing of good in it. *I was right,* they said, *neither do we;* asking, *wherein do you further differ from them?* I proceeded, that they held it needful to take, at certain times, a piece of bread to eat, with a small quantity of wine to drink after it is consecrated, as they call it, which they pretend to do in remembrance of Christ our Savior, urging this as necessary to our future happiness, as the former, calling this the Lord's supper. He told me, they had seen both these ceremonies put in practice by the Presbyterians, but could not understand, that if it was a supper, why they used it in the middle of the day; but they looked upon them both as very insignificant to the end proposed.

(*Jour.,* 1805, pp. 126-8)

It might be said that another feature of the doctrine of simplicity is the omission of a peculiar building in which to hold church services. What is a "church"? John Roberts gives the Quaker answer:

Bishop: . . . You are here returned (arraigned) for not coming to church. What say you to that?

J.R.: I desire to see my accusers.

Bishop: It is the minister and church wardens. Do you deny it?

J.R.: Yes, I do; for it is always my *principle* and *practice* to go to church.

Bishop: And do you go to *church?*

J.R.: Yes, and sometimes the *church* comes to me.

Bishop: The church comes to you? I don't understand you, friend.

J.R.: . . . I call the people of God the Church of God, wheresoever they are met to worship him in spirit and in truth.

(Jour., 1852, pp. 39-40)

The same point is made by Isaac Hopper (1771-1852): At Westminster Abbey he paid the customary fee of two shillings sixpence for admission. The doorkeeper followed him in, saying, "You must uncover yourself, sir." "Uncover myself!" exclaimed the Friend, with an affectation of ignorant simplicity. "What dost thou mean? Must I take off my coat?" "Your coat!" responded the man, smiling. "No indeed. I mean your hat." "And what should I take off my hat for?" he inquired. "Because you are in a church, sir." answered the doorkeeper. "I see no church here," rejoined the Quaker. "Perhaps thou meanest the house where the church assembles. I suppose thou art aware that it is the *people,* not the building, that constitutes a church?" . . .

(Jour., 1853, pp. 307-8)

Quaker peculiarities of behavior in their endeavor to dispense with superfluities would make a long list. These peculiarities can be found in a three volume work entitled: *A Portraiture of Quakerism, taken from a view of the moral education, discipline, peculiar customs, religious principles, political and civil economy, and character, of the Society of Friends,* by Thomas Clarkson, published in London (1806) and later in Philadelphia. Clarkson was not a Quaker himself, but he became intimately associated with Quakers in the anti-slavery movement in England. He says in his introduction that much has been written about the Quaker ideas but little about their peculiar behavior so he proposes to deal with this.

For example, he gives a long list of occupations which a consistent Quaker could not engage in, e.g., bookseller, goldsmith or silversmith, tailor. In these occupations a Quaker might be tempted to produce articles which were superfluous. A bookseller might find that he could not stay in business without selling fiction, a goldsmith without selling jewelry, and a tailor without making clothes for a new fashion before the old clothes were worn out. There were few who made such serious sacrifices in behalf of plainness of dress as did the Quaker tailors. Gilbert Latey (1626-1708) and John Hall (1637-1719) lost most of their business by refusing to make fashionable clothes. As Gilbert Latey had been a tailor at the King's Court he was sometimes able to help persecuted Quakers. Through his influence with the Catholic chaplain of the Queen-Mother, he secured freedom for two women traveling ministers imprisoned by the Inquisition in a dungeon on the island of Malta. At one time he found himself unexpectedly preaching in the royal Catholic Chapel and the chaplain expressed agreement with all he said. Warned that a certain meeting would be raided by soldiers, he was of course careful to be present at that meeting. Gilbert Latey was one of twelve Quaker tailors in London who wrote a powerful letter against superfluities in dress. The letter contains the words: ". . . being Taylors, in which we have met with many Tryals on every hand for many Years together . . . as being delivered from under those Burthens, that many yet groan under, and are not redeemed out of, as Lace, Ribbons, and needless Buttons, altogether useless; . . . . And as for the manner and way of answering the World in making their Cloaths, we leave it to the Witness of God in you all, and as much as in you lies beget them into Moderation. . . ."

(Jour., 1707, pp. 84-86)

John Woolman (1720-1772) expresses one reason why Friends attempted to do without all superfluities:

> Were all superfluities, and the desire of outward greatness laid aside, and the right use of things universally attended to, such a number of people might be supplyed in things usefull, as that moderate labour, with the Blessing of Heaven, would answer all good purposes relating to people and their Animals, and a Sufficient number have time to attend to proper Affairs of Civil Society.

(Jour., 1922, p. 404)

CHAPTER VIII

The Peace Testimony

IN my book *Friends for 300 Years* I have drawn a diagram (p. 120) which divides Quaker doctrines into three interdependent groups which might be called primary, secondary, and tertiary. These are not chronological in order, as any one of them may develop first and later produce the others.

The primary doctrine is that in every human being there is an inward Light or inward Life. The secondary testimonies are Meeting for Worship and Meeting for Business. In these, special attention is given to the leading of the Light and special effort is made to follow the leadings of the Light within the meeting community.

The tertiary testimonies—peace, equality, simplicty, and community—represent efforts to apply the doctrine of the Inward Light in the world outside the meeting in which special difficulties will be encountered. These four might be called "social testimonies" as compared to the others which are more definitely religious in character. But this distinction is artificial and they should be considered to be as definitely religious as the primary and secondary testimonies. The basis of all of them is the doctrine that the same identical Light is in all human beings. George Fox repeatedly asks Friends to answer "that of God" in other men. Robert Barclay says that the Light unites us to God and to one another. This summarizes the whole Quaker theology and philosophy.

The Quaker belief in peace is not just a negative refusal of war, but also an endeavor to appeal to "that of God" in other men regardless of nationality, race, or social status. This appeal may not at first appear successful, but it is the only appeal which can be successful in the long run.

The Journalists whom we are now considering have never, as far as I know, compromised on their peace principles and have consistently refused to have anything to do with war. They have also endeavored to create conditions under which war will not occur. No extensive portions of the Journals are devoted to the subject of war and peace, but all of them contain descriptions of encounters with persons who have views different from their own. Most include the assertion that the writer is willing to live as if the Kingdom of Heaven had arrived in himself since he believed that that is the only way the Kingdom can eventually come.

Joseph Hoag relates the following dialogue. It follows a long argument with a military officer. A man in his audience said: "Well, stranger, if all the world was of your mind, I would turn and follow after." Joseph replied: "So then thou hast a mind to be the last man in the world to be good. I have a mind to be one of the first and set the rest an example." (*Jour.*, 1861, p. 201)

Thomas Story (1666-1742) also, in an argument with a Baptist preacher, declares that the Society of Friends is willing to take the risk of being among the first in whom the Kingdom of Heaven begins.

> *The Kingdoms of this world shall all become the Kingdoms of our God and his Christ:* . . . But until this be finished by Degrees, as it is now begun and proceeds, the Kingdom of Christ on Earth is, and shall be, as at the first, a holy Nation, a Royal Priesthood, a peculiar People, zealous, not to fight and destroy, or to meddle with the Kingdoms or Rule of the World, but of good Works; against whom there is no Law, founded upon Righteousness and Truth: But, until this be accomplished, Nation will lift up Sword against Nation, and they will learn and exercise War: but as to us, we through the Mercy and Goodness of God, are of those in whom this Prophecy is begun to be fulfilled, and we can learn War no more.
>
> (*Jour.*, 1747, pp. 366-7)

In another argument, Peter the Great, Czar of Russia, during his visit to London asked Thomas Story: "Of what use can you be in any kingdom or government seeing you will not bear arms and fight?" Thomas replied:

He that commanded that we should love our Enemies, hath left us no Right to fight and destroy, but to convert them. And yet we are of Use, and helpful in any Kingdom or Government: For the Principle of our Religion prohibits Idleness, and excites to Industry; as it is written, *They shall beat their Swords into Plough-shares, and their Spears into Pruning-hooks:* . . . we, by so great an Example (the Lord Jesus Christ), do freely pay our Taxes to Caesar, who of Right, hath the Direction and Application of them, to the various Ends of Government, to Peace or to War, as it pleaseth him, or as Need may be, according to the Constitution or Laws of his Kingdom.

(Ibid., pp. 124-5)

Since Paul uses military metaphors, I can use one here. These Quakers are like small reconnaissance groups sent ahead of an army in order to explore the way and ascertain the presence and position of the opposing army. This is dangerous work but important if an advance is to be made. Thus the Quakers have quite properly been called perfectionists by Reinhold Niebuhr and others, not because they believe that they are perfect, but because they are often willing to take a position, however danger-ous, in advance of the social progress of humanity in general.

One question Quaker pacifists are frequently asked is: "What would you do if you were attacked by someone who threatened to kill you?" The following answer was given by Thomas Chalk-ley:

I being innocent, if I was killed in my body, my soul might be happy; but if I killed him, he dying in his wickedness, would, con-sequently be unhappy; and if I was killed, he might live to repent; so that if he killed me, I should have much the better, both in re-spect to myself and to him.

(Jour., 1754, pp. 207-8)

Since this is a controversial issue, I shall give another example from the Journal of Catherine Phillips, who is not quite as sure as Chalkley how she will react:

Once the subject of self-defense was started, which they might probably think we could not invalidate; but we were enabled to give a reason for dissenting from them in sentiment, and on its being queried what we would do if attacked, and must either be killed, or kill. I said I could not say how I should act at such a

juncture, wherein nature might be improperly raised; but that now
being favoured with the hope of my immortal spirit's centering
safe, and knowing that a person who sought my life must be in an
unfit state to enter Christ's holy kingdom, I should rather choose
to die, than plunge that soul into everlasting misery; and should
have greatly the advantage in being released from this state of trials.
They heard with attention, and the Swede with tears in his eyes,
replied, "These are indeed sublime sentiments."

(Jour., 1798, pp. 176-7)

Jonathan Dickenson (1663-1704) and his shipmates had a
chance to put their pacifism into practice. His Journal is entitled *God's Protecting Providence, Man's Surest Help and Defence in Times of Greatest Difficulty and Most Imminent
Danger, Evidenced in the remarkable Deliverance of Robert
Barrow, with divers other Persons, from the devouring Waves
of the Sea, amongst which they suffered shipwreck; and also
from the cruel devouring Jaws of the inhuman Cannibals of
Florida.* (First published in 1699.) On the day their ship ran
aground off the south-east coast of Florida, they were surrounded
by Indians with knives in their hands. "We stirred nor moved
not; but sat all or most of us very calm and still, some of us
in a good frame of spirit, being freely given up to the will of
God." The Indians were shouting and threatening, "But on a
sudden it pleased the Lord to work wonderfully for our preservation, and instantly all these savage men were struck dumb,
and like men amazed, for the space of a quarter of an hour, in
which time their countenances fell, and they looked like another
people." They looted the stores from the ship, stripped the
travelers and sailors of all but "a pair of breeches, or an old
coat" and left them. A week later,

> About sun-rising we saw the Indians coming, running in a very
> great number with their bows and arrows . . . they came in the
> greatest rage that possibly a barbarous people could, . . . We sat
> all still expecting death, and that in a most barbarous manner,
> . . . they rushed violently on us rending and tearing those few
> clothes we had: they that had breeches had so many about them,
> that they hardly touched the ground till they were shaken out of
> them. . . . After they had taken all from us but our lives . . . tak-
> ing their bows and arrows with other weapons, cried out *Nickaleer,*

Nickaleer (English, English) . . . drawing their arrows to the head. But suddenly we perceived them to look about and listen, and then desisted to prosecute their bloody design. One of them took a pair of breeches and gave it to my wife. We brought our great Bible and a large book of Robert Barclay's to this place . . . these cannibals took the books, and tearing out the leaves would give each of us a leaf to cover us.

(*Jour.*, 1945, pp. 43-6)

(The company reached New York seven months later, having traveled north from August 23, 1696 until April 1, 1697 by foot and canoe.)

Quaker ship captains found it difficult to obtain sailors because they refused to arm their vessels against pirates or privateers. Thomas Chalkley repressed a threatened mutiny by telling his sailors that if they killed any of those who attacked them, they would go to hell. This is, as far as I can remember, the only reference to hell in the Quaker Journals. Wooden imitations of real guns were called "Quaker guns."

Edward Coxere (1633-1694) was a gunner by trade, protecting the merchant ships of England during the Commonwealth and the Restoration, fighting for whatever flag was being flown. "Next I served Spaniards against the French, then the Hollanders against the English; then I was taken by the English out of a Dunkirker; and then I served the English against the Hollanders; and last I was taken by the Turks, when I was forced to serve them against English, French, Dutch, and Spaniards, and all Christendom. Then, when I was released from them, I was got in a man-of-war against the Spaniards, till at last I was taken prisoner by the Spaniards . . . and came home only my clothes to my back to my poor wife." (*Jour.*, 1946, pp. 37, 119) Four years and several voyages later (in 1661) he reports in his Journal:

I being now at home with my family, to spend some time till another freight presented, two men called Quakers came to our town at Dover, Samuel Fisher and Edw. Burows. William Rusell, a priest, and they were to have a dispute in James's Church, so called. . . . My mind being set to hear both parties, gave as good attention as I could, insomuch that the Lord at that time visited my soul and reached my very inward parts, so that my understanding was something opened, that my affections drew to the principle the Quaker held forth to be more sound than the priest's. Now there were many people hearers; I took notice of them, and such as I knew to be the rudest sort of people despised the Quakers and held with the priest. This confirmed me the more; the Lord let me see it to my farther convincement. This was not all, but the Lord in his mercy followed me that very day, and brought not peace but trouble; for the first remarkable opening I had before I slept from the Lord was concerning fighting or killing of enemies. The questioning of the lawfulness or unlawfulness of it lay on me as a very great burden, because it struck at my very life.

I got to Luke Howard's house in the evening, where these two men were to seek for ease, and told them I was a seaman and upon going to sea, we having wars, and should we meet with an enemy whether or no I might not lawfully fight. They, being very mild, used but few words, I being a stranger to them, but wished me to be faithful to what the Lord did make known to me, and words to that purpose, so did not encourage me to fight, but left me to the working of the power of the Lord in my own heart, which was more prevalent than words in the condition I then was in: so that I did not lay down fighting on other men's words, but the Lord taught me to love my enemies in his own time. . . . I saw that I had a very heavy cross to take up, and it was indeed: it was so heavy that I could not soon take it up; I was yet too weak.

(Ibid., pp. 129-131)

Two hundred years ago it was the custom to celebrate a victory in war by lighting up all the windows of the house. When the Quakers in Philadelphia refused to light their windows at the defeat of Cornwallis at Yorktown, during the Revolutionary War, many of their houses were seriously damaged by mobs. Elizabeth Drinker (1734-1807) wrote a journal about this period which was too long to print in its entirety. Cecil Drinker compiled portions concerned with living conditions, health, and medicine. (Not So Long Ago, A Chronicle of Medicine and Doctors in Colonial Philadelphia. New York: Oxford University Press, 1937.) Other excerpts, edited by Henry Biddle (Philadelphia: Lippincott, 1889) deal with the period of the American Revolution. The following quotation is taken from the second book of extracts:

1781   Oct. 19. . . . A mob assembled about 8 o'clock or before, and continued their insults until near 10, to those whose

Houses were not illuminated. Scarcely one Friend's House escaped. We had nearly 70 panes of glass broken; the sash lights and two panels of the front door broke in pieces—the Door cracked and violently burst open; when they threw stones into the House for some time, but did not enter. Some fared better and some worse. Some Houses, after breaking the door, they entered, and destroyed the Furnityre &c. Many women and children were frightened into fits, and 'tis a mercy no lives were lost.

(*Jour.*, 1889, p. 137)

The Quakers did not suffer for refusing to fight during the Revolutionary War. If they had been conscripted into the army, they would have been considered to have only a nuisance value. But many Quaker farmers, like other farmers, lost property through the depredations of both the British and American armies. Quakers generally, however, got along well with the British. My own ancestor, Edward Brinton, was visited by a group of British officers, probably with the intention of robbing his wine cellar. He told them that he thought the mother country had behaved very badly. They agreed with him.

The following dialog took place between George Washington and Warner Mifflin (1745-1798). Washington had met Mifflin some time earlier when Mifflin had walked through the dead on the battlefield of Germantown to carry a message to the Commander in Chief from the Yearly Meeting then in session.

The president recollected what Mifflin had said to him at Germantown, and thus addressed him: "Mr. Mifflin, will you please to inform me on what principles you were opposed to the revolution?" Mifflin answered, "Yes, friend Washington;—upon the same principle that I should be opposed to a change in this government. All that ever was gained by revolutions, are not adequate compensation to the poor mangled soldier, for the loss of life or limb." After some pause and reflection, the president replied, "Mr. Mifflin, I honour your sentiments;—there is more in *that,* than mankind have generally considered."

(*Jour.*, 1905, pp. 74-75)

During the French and Indian wars and the Revolutionary War, Friends had difficulty in making their minds up on the question of paying taxes. At both times there was a party in Yearly Meeting who believed that taxes could be paid "in the mixture," that is, if some of the taxes were used for peaceful purposes, while many prominent Friends were opposed to paying any taxes for war. John Woolman says:

> I all along believed that there were some upright-hearted men who paid such taxes, but could not see that their Example was a Sufficient Reason for me to do so, while I believed that the Spirit of Truth required of me as an individual to suffer patiently the distress of goods, rather than pay actively.
>
> *(Jour.,* 1922, p. 204)

Job Scott explains how to get along with a tax collector:

> I believe I was ever preserved in such meekness, as never to say or do any thing that raised anger or resentment in any of them. They ever heard me with attention, appeared unwilling to distress me, spoke to me in moderation, and left me without distraining anything from me. And although I could hear of their getting very warm and angry with some Friends who I feared were a little rough with them, they were constantly quite mild and gentle with me.
>
> *(Jour.,* 1831, p. 80)

Since the Yearly Meeting could not come into unity on this question, no decision was made that would apply to all Friends.

In Philadelphia Rebecca Jones, who had a school, refused to accept money from a British officer in return for teaching his children. The officer said that if she would not accept money, he would hang his coat on her fence and she could cut off the gold buttons in payment. This she also refused to do, though his children continued to go to her school.

In July 1863, a recently convinced Friend, Cyrus Pringle (1838-1911), was drafted into the Union Army. The diary of his experiences after his refusal to serve or pay for a substitute has recently been published by Pendle Hill. (Pamphlet 122, 1962):

> . . . we were urged by our acquaintances to pay our commutation money; by some through well-meant kindness and sympathy; by others through interest in the war; and by others still through a belief they entertained it was our duty. But we confess a higher duty than that to country.
>
> *(The Civil War Diary of Cyrus Pringle,* p. 8)

He was held in army camps and treated with great severity by officers who did their best to beat the Quaker out of him, until

President Lincoln ordered his release.

Allen Jay (1831-1910) in his Journal speaks of his refusal to pay $300 for a substitute. The military officer, after putting up notices that property would be sold to pay the fine, took dinner with Jay and his wife. After the dinner he said, "If you would get mad and order me out of the house, I could do this work much easier, but here you are feeding me and my horse while I am arranging to take your property from you. I tell you it's hard work." (*Jour.*, 1910, p. 96) Lincoln, having heard from the Governor of Ohio of Allen Jay's case, ordered that his property should not be sold. The Quakers in the South suffered severe persecution for refusing to enlist. But in the North, where more men were available, and President Lincoln and Secretary of War Stanton were sympathetic, there was less persecution.

The first World War resulted in a good deal of autobiographical material by Quakers. Two that could be called Journals are the *Autobiography* (1952) of Stephen Hobhouse (1881-1951) and *On Two Fronts* (1918) by Corder Catchpool (1883-1952). Both Hobhouse and Catchpool felt that alternative non-combatant service would not be sufficient protest against war and conscription. Both were drafted into the British army and then faced courts martial for disobeying orders. Hard labor so affected Stephen Hobhouse's health that, I remember, when he visited me in America he had to lie down while he talked. Corder Catchpool served three sentences, the second of which was reduced by half because he had been in the Friends' Ambulance Unit before he was drafted. After his release from a term at Wormwood Scrubs he wrote:

> The papers fascinate me—it is like coming out of a dark cellar into dazzling light (simile not a good one, in view of the present world obscurity!) which attracts and yet hurts. To me, to be shut off from news of the world is like being in ignorance of the welfare of a loved one, always worse than knowledge, even if the news be bad. . . . I seem hardly able even to pray intelligently unless I *know.*
>
> (*Jour.*, 1918, p. 159)

Quaker refusal to use violence in another type of situation is reported in the memoir of Philip Price (1764-1837), superintendent of Westtown School from 1818-1830.

When the men teachers all united in judgment that the conduct of a boy had been such that corporal punishment must be inflicted, they laid the case before the Superintendent. After hearing the statement of the teachers, he usually sat fifteen or twenty minutes with them in the most solemn stillness, and manifestly under an intense exercise and concern that a right judgment might prevail in the case; and I have known in repeated instances, the influence of his precious spirit so to operate upon the minds of the teachers, that, without his uttering a single word, they would unitedly propose a milder treatment; and, what it was very interesting to observe, there was not a single instance, where the milder course was adopted under these circumstances, which was not entirely satisfactory and successful in the result.

(Memoir of Philip and Rachel Price, 1852, pp. 164-5)

So far in the quotations from the Journals I have emphasized the negative side of the Quaker peace testimony, in other words, what Quakers have refused to do rather than what they do. In every war throughout Quaker history, Quakers have done relief work during and after the war. To describe all of this would take a large volume. One such volume—560 pages—has been written which takes the story of Quaker relief work up to 1920. (Margaret E. Hirst, *Quakers in Peace and War, an Account of their Peace Principles and Practice.* New York: Doran, 1923). The wide scope of Quaker relief work in both time and space is illustrated by the title of another book: *The Quaker Star Under Seven Flags.* (John Forbes, University of Pennsylvania Press: 1962).

Religious pacifism as a postive way of life rather than as a negative attitude toward fighting can be considered to be a direct derivative from worship. True worship which pierces through the surface of the mind where multiplicity lies, finds in the depths, beyond words and even thoughts, what George Fox called "the hidden unity in the Eternal Being." *(Jour.,* 1952 ed., p. 28) Here the worshiper feels as a present experience rather than as abstract theory his kinship with his fellow men in God. The early Friends seldom used the phrase "joined to the Lord" without adding its complementary expression "and to one another." Out of this unity comes a sensitizing of the soul, a feeling of oneness with all men which rules out conflict.

CHAPTER IX

Restriction of Business

There is the danger and temptation to you, of draw-ing your minds into your business, and clogging them with it; so that ye can hardly do any thing to the ser-vice of God, but there will be crying, my business, my business! and your minds will go into the things and not over the things" (George Fox in Epistle 131).

ALMOST every Journal contains some reference to restric-tions on business. These restrictions are quite different from those described by Max Weber in *The Protestant Ethic and the Spirit of Capitalism* (New York: Scribner, 1930). Ac-cording to Weber, the Puritans believed that they were required by their religion to be diligent in business, that is, in their voca-tion or calling. But their religion did not encourage them to spend. Accordingly capital would accumulate for investment.

The Quakers' restraint in business arose because there were no professional ministers nor any professionals to look after the affairs of the Society. So if Friends carried on large busi-nesses, they would not have time to perform their religious duties. By the Quakers, diligence in business was not despised, but there was a stage in spiritual development when it was expected that something higher should take precedence over it. The most famous case of such restraint is that of John Wool-man. He says:

> The increase of business became my burthen, for though my na-tural inclination was towards merchandize, yet I believed Truth re-

quired me to live more free from outward cumbers.

(*Jour.*, 1922, p. 183)

Hundreds of similar quotations can be found in the Journals. Daniel Wheeler (1771-1840) was a prosperous seed merchant who found that his business was taking attention away from his religious concerns.

> As I have from time to time endeavored to dwell near, and abide in and under, the calming influence of his power, I have been led to believe that something sooner or later would be required as a sacrifice on my part. . . . I therefore fully believe that it will be most conducive to my present peace, as well as future well-being, entirely to give up the trade I am at present engaged in and retire with my family into a small compass.
>
> (*Jour.*, 1859, pp. 57, 58)

He spent some years in Russia, teaching the Russians how to farm, and he took a long journey to the Sandwich Islands and the islands of the South Pacific.

Thomas Shillitoe (1754-1836) speaks of an

> apprehension which at times presented to my mind, that the time was fast approaching, when I must be willing to relinquish a good business which I had helped to get together, and set myself more at liberty to attend to my religious duties from home. The language which my Divine Master renewedly proclaimed in the ear of my soul, was "Gather up thy wares into thy house for I have need of the residue of thy days."
>
> (*Jour.*, 1839, I:39)

The following Friends did not go so far as to give up their businesses entirely. William Evans, when offered a partnership in a large dry goods business, refused it:

> My present business, being small and one that I understood, was managed with ease. It required little capital and involved me in no engagements that I did not hold the means to meet; so that I was free from anxiety on that account, and at liberty to attend, unincumbered, appointments of the Society or any impression of duty to go to a meeting that I might have. . . . It seemed that if I pursued the prospect of adopting the proposed change of business, that I should be lost to religious society and to the works of religion in my own heart. . . . I looked forward with renewed

peace and satisfaction at the path and the business before me, though small, remembering that the earth is the Lord's and the cattle on a thousand hills.

(*Jour.*, 1870, pp. 30, 31)

John G. Sargent (1813-1883) records in his diary in fifth month, 1839:

On going to my brickfield I was thoughtful as to my partnership with Cartiot, and that my wood-burning business alone might be sufficient for me, and perhaps more to my spiritual advantage than being too much cumbered with business.

(*Jour.*, 1885, p. 10)

Joseph Pike speaks of the Light of Christ shining in the heart, inclining "the obedient to spiritual things . . . as will lead them into the moderation, and keep within the bounds of Truth, so as not to run into extremes in trading and dealing, &c." (F. L. XI:387)

Thomas Chalkley was accused of mixing trading on his ship and traveling in the ministry, but the fact that he was mobbed on one of the islands of the West Indies for speaking against slavery should free him from the accusation of being too much interested in trading.

So I went to my calling, and got a little money (a little being enough) which I was made willing to spend freely, in the work and service of my great master Christ Jesus.

(*Jour.*, 1754, p. 11)

In the following lines Whittier indicates the extent to which Chalkley was willing to sacrifice himself:

Or Chalkley's Journal, old and quaint,—
Gentlest of skippers, rare sea-saint!—
Who, when the dreary calms prevailed,
And water-butt and bread-cask failed,
And cruel, hungry eyes pursued
His portly presence mad for food,
With dark hints muttered under breath
Of casting lots for life or death,
Offered, if Heaven withheld supplies
To be himself the sacrifice.

Then, suddenly, as if to save
The good man from the living grave,
A ripple on the water grew,
A school of porpoise flashed in view,
"Take, eat," he said, "and be content.
These fishes in my stead are sent
By Him who gave the tangled ram
To spare the child of Abraham."
(Whittier: *Snowbound*. See Chalkley, *Jour.*, 1754, p. 86)

It seems strange today that teaching school would result in too much attention to making money. Martha Routh, whose school was too large for its quarters, describes how she went out to look at a larger house:

> . . . as I passed from room to room I was attended by a secret but clear intimation that I was not to entangle myself with a greater number of scholars than the house we already had would accommodate, so I entirely gave up the thought and found peace.
>
> (*Jour.*, 1822, p. 36)

Rebecca Jones writes in a letter to Esther Tuke: "Thou hast, doubtless, heard that I have shaken my hands from the gain of schoolkeeping." (*Memorials*, 1840, p. 187). David Hall had the same concern:

> I resigned my school . . . that I might be more at liberty to wait on such service as I might think myself called to.
>
> (F.L., XXX:97)

A descendant of the Robert Barclay who wrote the famous *Apology*, a theological defense of Quakerism, founded one of the "big five" banks in England. The Quaker Lloyds of Wales were responsible for one of the others. Since the Quakers quite early established an extraordinary reputation for honesty, they were frequently entrusted by other persons with money. John Barclay was offered a position as a lawyer in one of the Barclay banks. He writes of this offer as follows:

> On considering the subject of the business proposed to me to enter upon, I can acknowledge that I would this day sign the articles of clerkship, if I thought it right to do so; but I feel too much given up and dedicated in heart and mind to Him, who has all my life long blessed and helped me, for me to undertake this proposed occupation; and therefore I do trust that though my

relations may not approve of the decision, they will respect the motives.

(Jour., 1877, p. 51)*

Friends also felt that they must exercise care not to follow interests which would occupy too much of their time such as scientific research. One of those was William Allen (1770-1843), called "the Spitalfields genius," who at an early age became a Fellow of the Royal Society. He writes in his diary:

> I am persuaded that it was the intention of the beneficent Creator that the conveniences, &c, of this life should be enjoyed, but yet kept in subordination. Beware lest chemistry and natural philosophy usurp the highest seat in thy heart.
>
> (Jour., 1847, 1:18)

Dr. John Rutty, an Irishman, who wrote many well-known scientific books as well as religious essays and a history of Friends in Ireland, kept a diary at the same time. He frequently scolds himself for putting too much attention on material instead of spiritual things.

> Instituted an hour's retirement every evening, as a check to the inordinate study of nature.
>
> (Jour., 1796, p. 13)

> An evidence of a greater propensity to the tree of knowledge than to the tree of life: but I trust this hath been mended.
>
> (Ibid., p. 15)

> Lord, deliver from living to eat, drink, sleep, smoke, and study. . . . Moderation in my calling is witnessed: may it be extended to the two darling objects, natural history and the materia medica.
>
> (Ibid., pp. 9-10)

Dr. Rutty finished his "Materia Medica" in spite of these restraints he put on himself.

Many Quaker shop keepers voluntarily limited their stock for sale in line with the dictates of conscience. David Ferris tells what happened when he started to feel uneasy about selling rum.

---

* John Barclay was one of the few Englishmen who understood why John Wilbur and his followers separated from New England Yearly Meeting. Wilbur's Journal contains correspondence with Barclay.

> Being unwilling to lose the profits of this branch of business, I adopted an expedient to soothe my pain; which was to refuse selling it to such as I thought would make evil use of it. But this did not answer my expectations; for they would send for it by those who were not suspected. At length I was made to relinquish the profits made on this article; and trust to Providence for the result.

When he ceased to sell rum, as when he ceased to sell "superfluous articles such as gay calicoes; flowered ribbands, and other fine things," he found that it "made no great diminution of (his) business." (*Jour.*, 1855, pp. 58-59)

In 1798 John Comly received a pamphlet by Thomas Clarkson written to dissuade people from using West India sugar and rum "alleging that these products were dyed scarlet in the blood of the enslaved Africans." By 1810 Elias Hicks had offended quite a number of Friends by preaching against buying any material produced by slaves. Many limitations of business were caused by the Quaker testimony against slavery. The Journal of George Taylor (1803-1891) should be noted since it contains an account of the formation of the Free-labor Produce Association of Friends for the purpose of supplying stores with the products of free labor, especially sugar and cotton. Capital was raised with which to fund new machinery and a water-power mill so that a great variety of goods could be manufactured. The business lasted until the abolition of slavery in the United States.

> The closing of the mill and disposal of the machinery was attended with much perplexity and heavy loss, which, however, fell lightly on me, from the kindness of all the large subscribers to the machinery. They agreed to lose what they had contributed. My loss was several thousand dollars.
>
> (*Jour.*, 1891, pp. 42-3)

In dealing with Quaker financial concerns, mention should be made of the way each Meeting assists its members who are in need, but references to these activities are to be found more in the Monthly Meeting minute books than in the Journals. The attitude of the Quaker Journalists as a whole might be summed up in these words from the Journal of Christopher Story (1648-1720):

About this Time, my Heart came to be more and more opened, and I saw the Danger of Poverty and Riches, and at a certain Time, I retired, and the Saying of the *Wiseman* came into my Remembrance, and I prayed to the Lord, to give me neither Poverty nor Riches, for I saw there was Danger on both Hands.

(Jour., 1726, p. 8)

CHAPTER X

Other Social Testimonies

WE have discussed the testimony for plainness in speech, dress, and behavior. We have also discussed the peace testimony, and Friends' curtailment of business. Most of the Journalists, in addition to having a concern to travel in the ministry, were concerned with the principal social problems of their time. Among these were the welfare of Indians, abolition of slavery and the care and education of slaves after they were freed, reform of prisons and mental hospitals, and relief of the poor. Education also has been a prime concern of the Society of Friends. I have already attempted to deal with this subject at some length in *Quaker Education* (Pendle Hill: 1967). In all of these concerns the Quakers were often among the first to act, as is indicated by the title of a book by Auguste Jorns, *The Quakers as Pioneers in Social Work* (New York: Macmillan, 1931). And here, as in the vocal ministry, women participated on a basis of equality with men from the beginning of the Society. George Fox maintained that: "Man and Woman were helps meet in the Image of God" (*Epistles,* 1698, p. 323).*

---

* Edward Hicks declares humorously:

Dear Martha Smith presented to my mind a case . . . which exhibits in a clear view, the great importance of superior women always being right, for when they get wrong they are so difficult to manage. This the apostle Paul experienced in the Corinthian church, and did what he thought was the best thing at that time, by commanding them to be silent; and I think it was well for me that I had not Paul's influence and authority, as I think I should have made bad use of it.

(*Memoirs,* 1851, p. 136)

The Society of Friends has maintained lobbies to influence legislation from their earliest days up to the Friends Committee on National Legislation which is active in the United States today. The first important lobby was led by William Penn and George Whitehead in the 17th century. This lobby was established not only to influence the members of Parliament but also their constituents. Thomas Scattergood (1748-1814) relates how a committee of four Quakers traveled to Lancaster, Pennsylvania, in 1808 to persuade the legislature not to pass a bill requiring Quakers to serve in the militia. When the committee arrived, one of the legislators was in the midst of condemning Quaker pacifism.

> Whilst this uncalled for and unwarranted defamation was at its height, the four Friends entered the hall. No sooner did the declaimer behold his much respected friend and near neighbor, Thomas Scattergood, among his auditors, than he found his spleen against the Quakers subside,—he admitted their good qualities, and, warming to their virtues, he ended by a complete eulogium on them. The mirth of the house was excited at the sudden change wrought in the orator by the entrance of the committee, and when this section of the bill came to be considered, there appeared a disposition unmanifested before by many of them, as well as by the orator, to think well of Friends, and to respect their wishes.
>
> (*Jour.*, p. 464)

Concern for the Indians began with Fox and Penn. The Puritans treated the Indians as if they were wild beasts having no sense of right or wrong. In his Journal George Fox describes an argument with the Governor of the Carolinas in which a doctor denies that the Indians have "the light and spirit of God."

> . . . he so opposed it in every one, that I called an Indian . . . and I asked him if that he did lie and do that to another which he would not have them do the same to him, and when he did wrong was not there something in him, that did tell him of it, that he should not do so, but did reprove him. And he said there was such a thing . . . that he was ashamed of them.
>
> (*Jour.*, 1952 ed., p. 642)

In 1793, some Indians in northern Ohio sent to Philadelphia asking Quakers to come to them to help in making a treaty.

(When treaties were made, the Quakers always tried to have a representative present if the Indians requested it.) William Savery (1750-1804), one of the five persons sent, records in his Journal the letter addressed to the Indians by Philadelphia Yearly Meeting. I shall quote only a part of that long letter.

> Brothers,—Our grandfathers told your grandfathers, that the Great and Good Spirit who made them and all people, with a design that they might live on this earth for a few years, in love and good-will one toward another, had placed his law in the hearts of all men, and if they carefully attended to its inward voice, it would keep them in love and friendship, and teach them to shun everything that would occasion them to trouble and hurt one another.
>
> (*Jour.*, 1863, p. 30)

After Grant was elected President, he was visited by a group of Friends who were concerned about the condition on the Indian reservations. Grant said that if they would send him a list of Quakers who could act as agents on the reservations, he would appoint them. Some of these Indian agents wrote Journals. Thomas Battey (1826-1897) whose Journal has recently (1968) been reissued in its entirety by the University of Oklahoma, reports this incident:

> . . . I noticed an old Indian in the dining-room, of a full, open countenance, wrapped in a buffalo robe, after the wild Indian style, watching me. As that was no new occurrence, however, I thought nothing of it, until he spoke to me by the interpreter. I went to him, and he said, "My friend, I can see your heart." This salutation, coming from a wild Comanche, somewhat startled me, particularly as at the time I was much depressed, feeling that there was no good thing there. After a little pause he continued, "Tell him I see his heart, it good—full of love; he love Indian; I can never hurt man when I see heart like his—full of love—I love him. . . ." I could but believe his heart was touched by a power above his own, and that in him I should find a friend who might be of use to me in the ordering of future events.
>
> (*Jour.*, 1875, p. 42)*

---

* Two Journals kept by Quaker delegates to the Indians of New York have now been published by The American Philosophical Society as part of a project for the political and cultural history of the Iroquois.

John Philips: A nineteenth century journal of a visit to the Indians of New York. Proc. Amer. Philos. Soc. 1956. 100:582.

The Quakers in dealing with a defeated people, were attempting to teach the Indians to help themselves. Friends' Indian Schools first appeared in western New York in 1796, in Ohio in 1822, in Kansas in 1837, in Maine about 1850, and in North Carolina in 1880. The only one of these schools to survive to the present time is the school at Tunessassa in western New York. In his Journal James Henderson (1859-1942) relates some of his experiences at Tunessassa where he was superintendent from 1889-1894.

Almost every Journal written before the United States Civil War reports an active concern against slavery. In 1743 the Yearly Meeting decided that Friends should no longer buy imported slaves. By 1776, holding a slave became a disownable offense. In the same year the Declaration of Independence proclaimed that "all men are created equal."

The Journal of Benjamin Lundy (1789-1839), compiled by his children and edited by Thomas Earle, principally from autobiographical materials, contains a vivid account of the early years of the anti-slavery movement. Lundy distributed his newspaper, *The Genius of Universal Emancipation*, over the United States and Mexico. He advocated the resettling of slaves who wished it in Mexico, Haiti, or Liberia. He makes the following comment on the destruction of his printing press in 1838:

> Well! my papers, books, clothes—everything of value (except my journal in Mexico, &c.) are all, *all* gone—a total sacrifice on the altar of Universal Emancipation. They have not yet got my *conscience,* they have not taken my *heart,* and until they rob me of these, they cannot prevent me from pleading the cause of the suffering slave.
>
> "The tyrant (may even) hold the body bound,—
> But knows not what a range the spirit takes."
>
> I am not disheartened, though every thing of earthly value (in the shape of property) is lost. Let us persevere in the good cause. *We shall assuredly triumph yet.*
>
> (*Jour.,* 1847, p. 303)

It was Lundy who, in 1828, converted William Lloyd Garrison to the cause of emancipation.

Halliday Jackson's Journal of a visit paid to the Indians of New York. Proc. Amer. Philos. Soc. 1957. 101:565-588.

Before the Emancipation Proclamation many Friends helped
to run the so-called "underground railroad." Levi Coffin (1798-
1877) was so active in this undertaking that he was called "the
President of the Underground Railroad." His Journal contains
many stories of the means by which slaves obtained their freedom.

> Eliza Harris of "Uncle Tom's Cabin" notoriety . . . was sheltered
> under our roof and fed at our table for several days. . . . She said
> she was a slave from Kentucky. . . . Her master got into some
> pecuniary difficulty, and she found that she and her only child were
> to be separated. . . . She watched her opportunity, and when dark-
> ness had settled down and all the family had retired to sleep, she
> started with her child in her arms and walked straight toward
> the Ohio river. She knew that it was frozen over, at that season
> of the year, and hoped to cross without difficulty on the ice, but
> when she reached its banks at daylight, she found that the ice had
> broken up and was slowly drifting in large cakes. . . . In the
> evening she discovered pursuers near (where she was hiding) and,
> with desperate courage she determined to cross the river, or perish
> in the attempt. . . . Clasping her babe to her bosom with her
> left arm, she sprang on to the first cake of ice, then from that to
> another and another. Sometimes the cake she was on would sink
> beneath her weight, then she would slide her child on to the next
> cake, pull herself on with her hands, and so continue her hazar-
> dous journey. She became wet to the waist with ice water and her
> hands were benumbed with cold, but as she made her way from
> one cake of ice to another, she felt that surely the Lord was pre-
> serving and upholding her, and that nothing would harm her. . . .
>
> In the summer of 1854 I was on a visit to Canada, accompanied
> by my wife and daughter. . . . At the close of a meeting which we
> attended, at one of the colored churches, a woman came up to my
> wife, seized her hand, and exclaimed: "How are you, Aunt Katie?
> God bless you!" etc. My wife did not recognize her, but she soon
> called herself to our remembrance by referring to the time she
> was at our house in the days of her distress, when my wife gave
> her the name Eliza Harris. . . . We visited her at her house while
> at Chatham, and found her comfortable and contented.
>
> (*Jour.*, 1880, pp. 147-50)

We do not have a Journal of Isaac Hopper, but his life,
written by L. Maria Child (Boston: Jowett, 1853) contains many

stories he told of stratagems used to help escaping slaves. In one case a slaveholder, disguised in Quaker costume, discovered where his escaped slave was located. Isaac Hopper was sent for to give help. The arrival of a constable and the slaveholder with a warrant to search the house attracted a large crowd of Negroes in front of it. In the house, Isaac Hopper asked that the door be opened. Immediately the curious crowd rushed in and then, when they were ordered out, the escaped slave left with them. Later Friend Hopper, as he was called, took the escaped slave to his house and then sent her out into the country. When the slaveholder asked Hopper where his slave was, he was answered that she was doing well and no more trouble needed to be taken on her account. The slaveholder replied: "The devil himself couldn't catch a slave in Philadelphia." "That is very likely," answered Friend Hopper, "but I think he would have less difficulty in catching the masters; being so much more familiar with them" (*Isaac T. Hopper; A True Life*, 1853, p. 192).

Elizabeth Comstock (1815-1891), the greatest part of whose Journal is concerned with the visiting of soldiers during the Civil War and work with the freedmen afterwards, recalls a few incidents connected with escaping slaves. At one time a Friend who was working with his pitchfork in the cattle yard, quickly hid an exhausted slave in a pile of straw just as his pursuers came to the gate. They demanded to know what had become of their "nigger." A sudden deafness seemed to have seized the farmer. They came closer, shouting louder. The farmer looked up and, with his hand behind his ear, asked: "Lost a cow, did you say?" "No, a nigger!" "Did she have a white spot on her forehead, Alderney breed?" "No, you old fool!" they shouted and tried to make him understand that they intended to search his house and buildings for their lost property. At length the farmer replied that he did not think an honest man needed to be afraid of having his house searched, and when the pursuers finally left, having looked into every nook and cranny, including the clock case, the Friend remarked, "Pity you didn't take the word of an honest man. I told you he wasn't there." Near the gate they saw one of the farmer's sons and asked if he had seen the Negro. The youth, like most Friends' children in those parts, was not disposed to help a slave catcher and replied that he had seen such a man going up a hill about a mile away an hour ago. This sent the pursuit on its way. The fugitive stayed quietly with the Friends for several weeks before going on to Canada by the underground railway (*Jour.*, 1895, pp. 64-66).

The concern of Edward Stabler (1769-1831) for the "destruction of the character, the humanity, and the morals of the country" was directed even more toward the slaveholders than the slaves:

> In my late religious journey over the peninsula of the Eastern Shore, I did indeed observe—as I have done whenever I have travelled, or been present in a country where slavery was practiced —that it not only tended to produce outward poverty by preventing improvements, and deterioration of the lands, but that it produced a still more disastrous penury in the minds of the slaveholders, by divesting them of those mental qualities upon which we are all dependent for comfort, and the want of which cannot be compensated by even the revenues of the world. . . . I have long been of the persuasion that much of the good that might have been done, has been obstructed by the attempts which have been made to abolish slavery, having originated and been prosecuted upon political, instead of religious motives and convictions. . . . They have seen, in so prominent an aspect, the wrongs and sufferings of the *slave,* that the still greater calamities of the master have been scarcely noticed. . . . As a consequence of this mode of proceeding, the slaveholder has considered himself injuriously assailed,—his mind has become exasperated, and he has placed himself upon the defensive, or become an assailant in his turn; and the result has been, that, like all other political contentions, the conflict has been degraded into a combat of persons, instead of a contest between the *principles* of right and wrong.
>
> (*Jour.*, 1846, pp. 109-110)

My Anti-Slavery Reminiscences by Elizabeth Buffum Chace (1806-1899) have been printed in a book of diaries entitled *Two Quaker Sisters* (New York: Liveright, 1937). Among many anecdotes and accounts of the family's anti-slavery activities, she includes the recollections of her sister, Rebecca Buffum Spring, who visited John Brown twice before his execution. "Although she had never met John Brown . . . she felt that she must go to see him and try to ease his path, which all knew, was now only to death. She felt that John Brown and his men had, although unwisely, taken the first positive step toward ending the impossible conditions under which the country was laboring." (pp. 166-7) The description of these visits is dramatic and affecting but too long to be included here. It has been reprinted in *The Quaker Reader* compiled by Jessamyn West (New York: Viking, 1962).

Many thousands of Negroes who were freed by the war were destitute and in much need of help. A freedman's association, formed by Friends of Philadelphia Yearly Meeting distributed clothing and food in the camps where Negroes collected and also set up schools in many parts of the South. Philadelphia Yearly Meeting alone started about forty schools and other Yearly Meetings were engaged in this work. The Freedman's Association of Philadelphia was not disbanded until about 1933.

Elizabeth Comstock was busy in many phases of post-war work. A letter to her sister is quoted in her Journal.

> Mrs. Comstock went a few weeks ago, at the request of the Governor of this State, to Illinois, and held a meeting in Farwell Hall, in the city of Chicago, to try to induce the people of that State to open the way for large numbers of these coloured emigrants that are literally filling Kansas to overflowing. The result of her meeting there was very satisfactory, as the people in that State resolved to take 50,000 of the coloured emigrants, and assist them in getting places of employment. After her return from Illinois, she went to Nebraska, at the request of the Governor, and has succeeded in turning some of the tide of emigration into that State. It is now contemplated making another headquarters for relief at a point in Nebraska, called White Cloud, which lies near the line of three States, Kansas, Nebraska, and Missouri. It is impossible to find homes and employment for the large coloured population that are coming.
>
> *(Jour.,* 1895, pp. 377-8)

A new epoch in treating the insane began in 1792 when William Tuke founded the York Retreat. Before this time the insane were chained and whipped, but at the York Retreat they were treated as far as possible like guests of a hotel. Samuel Tuke (1784-1857), the grandson of the founder, writes in his diary for fifth month 8th, 1813:

Received from the printer a copy of my *Description of the Retreat*. This work was commenced under a deep sense of the sufferings of the insane. Their afflictions have often been present with me in my retirement before God, and my prayer has been that for the poor and needy who have no helper, He would arise. May He prosper this imperfect effort to awaken the public sympathy towards them!

(*Life,* 1900, p. 48)

At least three hospitals similar to the Retreat were founded by Quakers in America. One, in Philadelphia, once called the Frankford Asylum (now the Friends' Hospital), in 1817; another in New York, founded by Thomas Eddy, called Bloomingdale (1821); and a third in Towson, Maryland, called Sheppards (1853). At the Pennsylvania Hospital, founded by two Quaker brothers named Bond, mental patients were medically treated for the first time.

Throughout the history of the Society of Friends there has been frequent concern for the condition of prisoners. The most famous prison reformer, and the most successful, was Elizabeth Fry (1780-1845). Her Journal has been published, with occasional additional commentaries, by her daughters (two volumes, 1847 & 1848). As her work is so well known, I shall move on here to some accounts from the lesser known Journals of Stephen Grellet and Thomas Shillitoe.

Stephen Grellet, in traveling through Russia, was shocked by the terrible conditions he saw in prisons where men were chained and loaded with irons for small offenses. The Czar, Alexander I, asked Stephen Grellet what he thought of the prisons.

We were glad to have the opportunity to acquaint him with the wretched situation of several of these, and of the poor-houses also. We alluded especially to the prison at Abo; we showed him the sketch, taken there of a man with his fetters upon him. The Emperor was much affected, and said, "These things ought not to be; they shall not continue so."

(*Jour.,* 2d American ed., p. 410)

Stephen Grellet also visited the Papal prisons and houses of correction in Rome. Afterwards he had an interview with Pope Pius VII, who admitted that reformation of these was necessary, so that Christian tenderness and care be exercised; means, as he said, more likely to succeed to promote reform among (prisoners) than harsh treatment.   (*Ibid.*, p. 555)

On the subject of the Inquisition, the Pope was pleased that Grellet had seen what great changes had been brought about in Rome.

> (The Pope) has made many efforts to have similar alterations introduced into Spain and Portugal. . . . He assented to the sentiment that God alone has a right to control the conscience of man, and that the weapons of a Christian should not be carnal but spiritual.   (*Ibid.*, p. 556)

(Stephen Grellet's hat was removed before the interview so quietly that he could not prevent its going.)

Thomas Shillitoe (1754-1836) twice visited a German prison at Spandau. He indicates in his Journal that he was a timid man, but in carrying out the concerns laid upon him, he was fearless. Having secured permission to visit the prison, he started out after removing his money, watch, pocketbook, and penknife so that they would not put temptation in anyone's way. Realizing that this was evidence of a lack of dependence on Divine protection in his mission, he returned to his room and restored these articles. When he arrived at the prison, the Governor of the prison was shocked to hear that Shillitoe wanted to meet all of the prisoners together. A former Governor had been murdered there and Shillitoe was warned that it would be very dangerous to get three or four hundred prisoners together in one place, all of them hardened men "whose legs were loaded with irons, but not their hands." "Had they been disposed to have injured us . . . we should only be like so many grasshoppers among them" (*Jour.*, 1839, II:48).

To the astonishment of the Governor, Shillitoe desired to go down among the prisoners and shake the hand of each one.

> I cannot call to remembrance a time when I have found a more open door to receive what was communicated, than in this opportunity; the countenances of many of the prisoners appeared sorrowfully affected, and bathed in tears; and the quiet solid manner in which they behaved during the whole of the meeting, con-

sidering what a rough, uncultivated company they appeared to be, was a striking proof of the sufficiency of the power of God, now as formerly, to control and bring into subjection, the evil power in man.

(Ibid.)

As a result of Shillitoe's visit, a society was formed in Berlin "for instructing and amending the prisoners."

Shillitoe showed the same inspired courage in visiting six hundred drinking places in Ireland and holding a Quaker Meeting in each one of them. He was usually treated well, although sometimes beer was thrown in his face. These visits were not apparently made in the cause of temperance but because of the scenes of serious depravity which he witnessed at these drinking places.

On a trip to Washington he visited a very vicious man surrounded by fierce dogs whose profession it was to tame rebellious slaves. He records an amiable, loving talk with this man, who was led to condemn his profession and to declare that he intended to give it up. (Jour., 1839, II:257-9) Afterwards, Shillitoe visited with President John Quincy Adams. It is surprising with what ease Friends secured interviews with Presidents, Czars, and Kings. Shillitoe began his career by visiting George III of England. It was the policy of traveling ministers to deal with the head of a nation whenever possible rather than with those of lesser importance.

Thomas Shillitoe has been classified by Quaker historians as a Quietist. Quietism is the doctrine that every self-centered trait or activity must be suppressed or quieted in order that the divine may find unopposed entrance to the soul. When he was considering, with much apprehension and fear, the prospect of a journey to Europe, he wrote:

If I remained willing to become like a cork on the mighty ocean of service, which my great Master should require of me, in the storm and in the calm, free from the lead of human reason, not consulting and conferring with flesh and blood, willing to be wafted hither and thither, as the Spirit of the Lord my God should blow upon me, he would care for me every day and every way; so that there should be no lack of strength to encounter all my difficulties.

(Ibid., I:230)

CHAPTER XI

Quakers and Animals

Thomas Clarkson in his Portraiture of Quakerism *says: The word benevolence, when applied to the character of the Society, includes also a tender feeling towards the brute creation. It has frequently been observed by those who are acquainted with its members that all animals belonging to them are treated with a tender consideration and not permitted to be abused; and that they feel in like manner for those which may be oppressed by others (III:131).*

THE QUAKER opposition to oppression was primarily based on a conscience sensitive to the Inward Light, the ultimate source of moral and religious insight. This was sometimes supplemented by appeals to reason and to the Scriptures. Since the Inward Light was believed to be in all men, every man should be treated in a way that permits an "answering" of the Light in him to the Light in others.

Quakers were not sure about the presence of the Light in animals. George Fox says of the beasts of the field "what they know they know naturally. But all (men) knowing one another in the Light . . . this differs you from the Beasts of the Field and from the World's Knowledge" (Epistle 149).

Hinduism and Buddhism have gone farther than Quakerism in their doctrine that all life is one and therefore, to injure any living creature, is to injure one's self. Buddhism insists that there is some measure of Buddha nature in every animal and insect and that this creature, if it permits the Buddha nature to be enlarged and grow, will be promoted to a higher plane of life, to that of a human being, perhaps, then to that of a celestial being, and finally to Buddhahood. We find, however, little if any of this feeling in Quaker writings, though Quaker theology, founded as it is so largely on the first chapter of John's gospel —where we are told that the Logos, the Word of God, is the creative power in the world—might permit us to assume that this Light, which is the Life of all men, is in some degree manifest in all created things. In spite of the lines quoted from George Fox, it is a short step to go on to the belief that in some degree the same Light shines in and through animal life.

Edward Burrough, a contemporary of George Fox and a prominent Quaker minister, considered that man in the Fall had his vision so dimmed and distorted that he had no clear conception of nature and its harmony, but that the man who is restored, the spiritual Christian, has a new and clear vision which leads him to see the creatures as they really are and to treat them as they should be treated. (*A Standard Lifted Up and an Ensign Held Forth to All Nations,* 1653, Chap. xv). George Fox felt that his vision of creation was so clarified, because he had come into the condition of Adam before the Fall, that he could see into the nature of plants and animals (*Jour.,* 1952 ed., p. 27). *The First Publishers of Truth* records that the writer of the account of the beginning of the Quaker movement in Worcestershire in 1655 commented on this:

> In our discourse together on the road before our parting (Fox) spoke of the glory of the first body and of the Egyptian learning and of the language of birds and of what was wonderful to me to hear, so that I believed he was of a deep and wonderful understanding in natural but especially in spiritual things.
>
> (*First Publishers of Truth,* p. 278)

Joshua Evans spoke of creation before the Fall as like that "day spoken of by the prophet Isaiah in which there was none to hurt or destroy in all God's holy mountain." (*Jour.,* 1837, p. 28) Before the Fall, he says "All the Lord's works were in harmony." Christ came to restore the condition before the Fall, but it was a higher condition according to Fox, since it was not based on innocence. Christ introduced a new order of spiritual awareness. Elizabeth Collins (1755-1831) writes regarding the time of her dedication to religious service:

> I also felt a great yearning of heart toward my fellow creatures and much tenderness and compassion for the brute creation.
>
> (*Jour.*, 1859, p. 21)

John Comly as a boy, after much trouble in saving money to buy a gun, found he could not use it in "shooting innocent animals for amusement." He justifies killing animals for food under necessity, but not hunting for pleasure, which he says "induces hardness of heart in the infliction of unnecessary pain, misery, and suffering upon many harmless animals" (*Jour.*, 1853, pp. 25, 26).

Joseph John Gurney, for similar reasons, renounced field sports. "I have," he says, "often taken great delight in the pursuit of them but am in my heart convinced that they are morally wrong" (*Jour.*, 1854, p. 40).

To take a modern example of this concern, we find in the autobiography of Stephen Hobhouse that because of the suffering he caused, especially because he was a poor shot, he gave up hunting early in his youth.

> I have felt, more and more as the years go by, my kinship with animals (even with the little creatures I had to destroy as a gardener) and my compassion for them when unkindly treated by men. I am strongly opposed to vivisection and my vegetarian diet is due to feelings of kinship with them as well as to reasons of health.
>
> (*Jour.*, 1952, p. 30)

Other Friends have become vegetarians for humanitarian as well as for hygienic reasons. In a record compiled by Arthur Brayshaw in 1941 from a variety of sources, the names of 76 Friends are listed as having been known to be vegetarians. Today many hundreds more might be added to the list.

Joshua Evans in his Journal wrote:

> My spirit was often bowed in awful reverence before the Most High and covered with feelings of humility and tenderness, under

which I had to believe that we ought to attend to Divine instruc-
tion, even in disposing of and governing the inferior part of his
creation that all our actions might be done as much as may be
to the Lord's honour. I considered that life was sweet in all living
creatures, and taking it away became a very tender point with me.
The creatures, or many of them, were given, or as I take it, rather
lent us to be governed in the great Creator's fear. . . .

I believe my dear Master has been pleased to try my faith and
obedience by teaching me that I ought no longer to partake of
anything that had life.

(Jour., 1837, pp. 27, 38)

Abuse of animals has always been cited as evidence of other
deficiencies of character. For example, William Allen writes:

There appears to me such a meanness and lowness of disposition
in those who are cruel to animals that I think I could not put
confidence in them, even in the common concerns of life.

(Jour., 1847, I:9)

And John Churchman recounts the following incident from his
boyhood:

I remember that a person once at my father's who spake about
religious matters with an affected tone, as if he was a good man;
when he went away I was near him, and when he mounted his
horse, taking a dislike to some of his motions, he called him an
ugly dumb beast, with such an accent as bespoke great displeasure
and grieved me much; for I did believe that man whose mind
was sweetened with divine love truly, would not speak wrathfully,
or diminutively, even of the beasts of the field.

(Jour., 1779, p. 4)

Instances of kindness to animals are infrequent in Quaker
Journals, probably because they were considered normal and
unworthy of record. Instances of cruelty, on the other hand, having a degrading effect on man's spirit, are most likely to be
mentioned. John Woolman in his Journal vividly recalls his
remorse for having killed a robin with a stone. This was at the
age of seven. He says, having been "seized with horror" for
killing "an innocent creature while she was careful of her
young," he climbed the tree and killed the young so that they
would not "pine away and die miserably." Here he discovered
how one cruelty can involve another *(Jour.,* 1922 ed., p. 152-3).

John Comly remembered a similar experience. At the age of four or five he killed a chicken by hitting it with a stone. He says that as he watched the dying chicken, "Horror and sorrow seized my infant soul. My heart then learned to feel tenderness toward every living thing that could feel pain and in all my childish sports and plays to avoid wanton cruelty" (*Jour.*, 1853, p. 5).

George Fox, in his account of his journey to Wales in 1657, says:

> And in that inn also I turned my back from the man that was giving oats to my horse and I looked back again and he was filling his pockets with the provender that was given to my horse, a wicked, thievish people to rob the poor dumb creature of his food, of which I had rather they had robbed me.
>
> (*Jour.*, 1952, p. 301)

At another time Fox, in the charge of "fifteen or sixteen men," was being taken under arrest to Lancaster. They forced him to ride on a "poor little horse."

> When they were come a pretty way out of the town they beat the poor little horse and made him kick and gallop. I lighted off him and told them they should not abuse the creature at which they mightily raged.
>
> (*Ibid.*, p. 376)

John Woolman was afflicted by the suffering of the barnyard fowls carried for food on the ship on which he made his journey to England. He believed that when the "love of God is verily perfected . . . we do not lessen the sweetness of life in the animal creation." In spite of this expression, John Woolman does not appear to have been like his neighbor and contemporary, Joshua Evans, a vegetarian. In England he would not travel by stage-coach or even send mail by it, because of the suffering of the stage boys, and the horses which were sometimes done to death by hard driving. (*Jour.*, 1922, p. 306)

An incident in the experience of Isaac Hopper is related in the account of his life:

> One day when he saw a man beating his horse brutally he stepped up to him and said, very seriously, "Dost thou know that some people think men change into animals when they die?"

The stranger's attention was arrested by such an unexpected question and he answered that he never was acquainted with anybody who had that belief. . . .

"But some people do believe it," rejoined Friend Hopper; "and they also believe that animals may become men. Now I am thinking that if thou shouldst ever be a horse, and that horse should ever be a man, with such a temper as thine, the chance is thou wilt get some cruel beatings." Having thus changed the current of his angry mood, he proceeded to expostulate with him in a friendly way; and the poor beast was reprieved, for this time at least.

(*Jour.,* 1853, p. 367)

Perhaps enough instances have been cited to show that a type of religion which has pioneered in such causes as anti-slavery, prison reform, non-violence toward the mentally ill, and help for the victims of war, inevitably results in sympathy for what we sometimes superciliously call the "brute creation." Whatever else man may have, he certainly has a body and instincts similar to those of beasts.

The most touching symbol of Christianity is the Lamb of God, and the lost sheep that was found is, perhaps, the most comforting of the parables. These have left their imprint on all Bible lovers. George Fox, who knew the New Testament by heart, had been a shepherd boy and throughout his long life he thought of his colleagues, even the most valiant of them, as "Dear Friends and Lambs." In a time of persecution he wrote to the sufferers:

So all Dear Lambs and Babes and Brethren, Happy and blessed are ye, who the seed do know, . . . who know the Shepherd and his Crook . . . he shews you the Pastures of Life in which ye must feed. . .

It may be, there will be a time of shearing and clipping (but) fear not losing the Fleece for it will grow again. Be faithful . . . laboring in love . . . some Threshing, some Ploughing, and some to keep the Sheep.

(*Epistles,* passim)

CHAPTER XII

Dreams of the Quaker Journalists

*Removing to another place I came among a people
that relied much on dreams. I told them, except they
could distinguish between dream and dream, they would
confound all together; for there were three sorts of
dreams; multitude of business sometimes caused dreams;
and there were whisperings of Satan in man in the night
season; and there were speakings of God to man in
dreams. But these people came out of these things and
at last became Friends (George Fox,* Journal, *1952 ed.,
p. 9).*

DREAMS belong in that shadowy borderland between fact
and fantasy where truth, if it appears at all, assumes
strange disguises. The early Quakers, more than any other group
of their time, distrusted imagination and made a consistent
effort to banish superstition. There are meeting records which
show that strong measures were taken with Friends who con-
sulted soothsayers or necromancers. No witches were condemned
in the Quaker colonies. In view of these tendencies, though many
dreams are recorded in the vast sum of Quaker religious autobiography, there generally appears a note of caution in regard
to credulity. George Fox cites, in the year 1647 at the beginning
of his ministry, the circumstances described in the quotation
which heads this chapter. His words may be taken as typical of
the Quaker attitude toward dreams. This attitude was not super-
stitious in the ordinary sense of that word, because the dreamer
as well as those to whom he communicated the substance of his

93

dream recognized that most dreams were not to be taken seriously. Nevertheless, for at least two hundred years, Friends felt that God does sometimes speak to man in dreams. For this they found ample Biblical precedent in the dreams of Jacob, Pharaoh, Nebuchadnezzar, Daniel, Joseph the husband of Mary, and many others. That some dreams may have profound significance is admitted by psychologists today.

Fox's three-fold classification of dreams was typical of the Quaker approach toward inward experiences in general. The early Friends believed that there is, within man, a super-human level of Divine Life, a human level of reason, and a sub-human level of sensual impulse. The lowest level could be described as diabolic if untempered by religion or enlightened reason. Inward intimations or impressions could come from any one of these three sources, and the man whose soul was properly sensitized through prayer and worship could distinguish one from the other. Dreams, like other types of inward revelation, bear within them the stamp of their origin. As we read the accounts of dreams in the Quaker Journals, we find that the dreamer is generally aware, even while he is dreaming, of the degree of importance of his dream. It is to be assumed, no doubt, that only those dreams are recorded which are felt to be important and of divine origin. Such a revelation might occur only once in a lifetime.

Many Journals contain no mention of dreams and few record more than two or three. Often a dream is mentioned with a note of apology, as, for instance, when Elizabeth Ashbridge writes, "Soon after I had a dream and though some ridicule dreams, this seemed very significant to me, and therein I shall mention it." (*Jour.*, p. 15) Thomas Story, each time he records a dream, is careful to remind us that it is only one of God's ways of speaking to man. "Now the dispensation of God," he says, "being various . . . he hath awakened and informed the mind, sometimes by Dreams, sometimes by Prophecy, sometimes by Signs, and at other times by immediate Revelation" (*Jour.*, 1749, p. 2).

Editors in preparing Journals for the printers, have sometimes omitted the dreams. For example, the original editors of the two most widely read Quaker Journals, those of George Fox and

John Woolman, omitted nearly all the dreams. Fortunately, these two Journals were famous enough to require later editions based on original manuscripts. The dreams of Fox can be found in the Cambridge edition of his Journal, 1911, and the dreams of Woolman in Amelia Mott Gummere's edition of his works, 1922. One is led to surmise that new editions of other Journals, based on original manuscripts, will disclose similar omissions by cautious editors.

The writers of Quaker Journals have, in general, leaned backward in attempting to avoid exaggeration or overstatement. It is fortunate that, in dealing with so controversial a subject as dreams, we have the testimony of writers who valued truth above all things, and who would put nothing in their Journals which contained for them any element of doubt.

Dreams, the interpretation of which is not evident, are seldom recorded. The Journalist is aware that the language of dreams is highly symbolic. The meaning of the symbols often becomes clear before the dreamer is fully awake, or at least soon afterward. Thomas Arnett writes:

> After I awoke my soul was gathered into the profoundest silence, the activity of thought was put to rest, every intervening cloud of imagination vanished and my soul centered in God, the eternal substance. While thus influenced, the instruction of the foregoing dream or vision was opened in the ear of my spirit.
>
> (*Jour.*, 1884, p. 25)

John Churchman had an elaborate dream of the flood and the resurrection of nature after it which received a complete interpretation in which every symbol was given a spiritual meaning. (*Jour.*, 1779, p. 217) The Journal writer usually offers at least a brief interpretation. Exceptions to this are sometimes due to the fact that the interpretation is obvious or that the dreamer was unable to interpret his dream.

In this chapter we shall, in general, accept the interpretations of the writers. It would be instructive, if space and ability permitted, to apply some of the methods of psychoanalysis to Quaker dreams. Jung, in particular, has thrown a brilliant light on dream analysis, supplementing the important initial findings of Freud. Quaker dreams are particularly interesting because dreams are essentially depth phenomena and Quakers, possibly more than other groups, have emphasized the importance of "going deep" or "centering down" where the soul may receive impressions of Truth from sources not accessible to conscious reason. The psychoanalyst, or analytical psychologist, endeavors to explore the depths which underlie the conscious area of the psyche. Such an investigator might differ from the Quaker on one important point. In his capacity as a purely scientific psychologist, he would probably find unnecessary the hypothesis that God uses these depths as an accessible channel for making His impress on the soul. There is, however, no good reason why a psychologist who is more than just a scientist might not regard this impress in the same way in which it is regarded by the writers of the Quaker Journals.

In many cases the Journalist does not know whether what he has seen is a dream or a vision; in other words, he does not know whether he was asleep or awake when the impression occurred. Quakers, especially while worshiping in the silence of a meeting, become very sensitive to impressions received without an exercise of the conscious will. Because there is no conscious volitional element involved, the line between visions and other kinds of impressions is sometimes difficult to draw.

W. H. R. Rivers, in his book entitled *Conflict and Dream* (New York: Harcourt, Brace, 1923) holds that a dream is usually a solution to a conflict, expressed in symbolic form. Many of the dreams recorded in Quaker Journals tend to bear out this thesis. They usually come at some crisis, when a difficult decision has to be made. Usually the conflict arises between weak, erring, human nature pulling in one direction and Divine Influence gently drawing in the other. The dreams which are worthy of record suggest an outcome favoring the Divine.

For example, Job Scott reports this dream at the conclusion of a period of conflict. It prophesies his decision to follow the Light without reservations.

> About four or five times, in a few months, I had the following dream, repeated nearly in the same manner. I beheld in my dream the sun nearly approaching the horizon, being just ready to set, sometimes in one part of the hemisphere, and sometimes in another. As it drew near setting, my soul was suddenly filled

with such awfulness and anxiety, as was scarcely supportable. A strong persuasion seized upon me, that now the world was to be instantly dissolved, and that I, altogether unprepared, should immediately launch into vast and endless eternity. Directly, upon this dreadful apprehension, the sun every time reached the earth; and as it apparently struck the earth, the fire kindled as in an instant, at the place where it struck, and passing over the earth's surface, almost as quick as lightning, would in a moment be surrounding close upon me; approaching with the utmost rapidity, as if no flesh was to escape immediate destruction, nor a single soul have time to think before death. In this terrible dilemma, I thought, I every time fell awfully on my knees and in the deepest anguish called on the name of the Lord, whom I had grievously offended, and begged aloud for mercy. Almost as soon as I was brought on my knees, in deep and true humiliation, the fire immediately all went out, and tranquility and peace were instantly restored. At this I awoke, I believe each time, almost overcome with joy, that I had escaped such imminent danger.

(Jour., 1831, p. 39)

Margaret Lucas, while her relatives were using violent means to prevent her from becoming a Quaker, dreamed that a man was separating wheat from chaff and that she was the chaff (*Jour.*, 1803, p. 41); James Dickinson dreamed that an evil man was attempting to drown a sheep, but a good man struggled with him and prevailed (F. L., XII:370); Joseph Hoag presents a vivid picture of himself standing before the Throne of Judgment (*Jour.*, 1861, p. 26); as also does Thomas Arnett (*Jour.*, 1884, p. 2). On another occasion, Arnett finds himself pursued in a dream by white horsemen, "their countenances pale as death, their appearance indescribably awful, looking at me with the keenest penetration" (*Ibid.*, p. 7). Sometimes this conflict appears in dreams as an effort to climb to a high place difficult of access. Jacob Ritter (1756-1841) tried in vain to climb a high tower by first entering an upper story with a ladder. Finally, he discovered that he must begin more humbly, in the basement (*Jour.*, pp. 53-54).

Hannah Bassett (1815-1853), in trying to climb a hill to a "spacious house" at the top, found herself continually falling back, but "there appeared to be someone present who constantly encouraged me not to give up" (*Jour.*, 1860, p. 48). Finally, she reached her goal. Allen Jay, in a conflict between allegiance to spiritualism or to Christianity, in a vision or dream, he does not know which, was attempting to get to the top of a high building but was constantly sidetracked by entering rooms given over to all sorts of studies and discussions. Finally, finding himself in complete darkness, "one like the Son of Man" appeared and led him to the top. (*Jour.*, 1910, pp. 33-36)

Jacob Ritter, while attempting to break with Lutheranism, dreamed that he saw a fire consume a church at the moment that its pastor stepped into the belfry in the presence of a great multitude. (*Jour.*, pp. 23-25) In a later dream, a Friend appeared and ordered him to go to a meeting which was assembling while he was asleep. This he did. (p. 56) John G. Sargent dreamed that he was "swiftly passing down a stream in a small boat without oars." Using his hands as oars he avoided numerous dangerous rocks and finally, though sometimes immersed in water up to his head, he arrived at a quiet harbor. On waking, he thought of this stream as typical of the Stream of Life. (*Jour.*, 1885, p. 28) Samuel Fothergill (1715-1772), speaking in meeting, told of a Friend who in early life was "concerned with his soul's salvation," but later "cared too much for the things of this life." He had a dream at each of these periods:

> The first was, his being placed in a fine green field or pasture, walled round, and several lambs feeding in it, well favoured and in good order, and in the midst a pure clear spring for them to drink at; that a sharp axe was given him with which to guard the well, that nothing should muddy it, and to keep up the wall, and if any breaches were made in it that he must repair them. The latter dream was, that he saw himself in the same field, but it had lost its verdure, the lambs were distempered and disordered, the wall much broken down, the water muddy, and serpents in it hissing at him, which he could not destroy or overcome, having lost the weapon formerly given him, and that as he stood looking at the lambs, he thought he heard a voice, saying "All these will I require at thy hands."
>
> (*Jour.*, 1844, p. 432)

No Quaker Journalist wrote of dreams with greater literary power than did Thomas Story. The two which occurred before and after his dedication to Truth are too long to quote, but they contain images expressive of awe and dread of the *mysterium tremendum*. Four bloody moons meet at the zenith and dash each other to pieces, while a dim sun retreats below the horizon. Then the stars appear and dash in violence against each other, falling to earth like "fruit from a tree shaken by a mighty hand." Darkness and horror descend on the earth. Now the dreamer resigns "all to the will of him who shaketh the Heavens" and immediately the scene is changed to an aspect of heavenly beauty. After the writer has thus resigned his will to God he sees in a later dream the Lord's army marching over the earth conquering without violence. Then comes a trumpeter who sounded the doom of all who would not repent. "Pale Death appeared on every face; the gay of the world were astonished and the mighty thereof trembled in great amazement and fear, but knew not where to hide themselves" (*Jour.*, 1747, pp. 2, 16, 17).

These dreams which symbolize and dramatize the conflict in the soul between good and evil nearly always prophesy victory for the Good.

Thomas Shillitoe, while endeavoring to decide whether or not he should further reduce his income so as to devote more of his attention to religious service, dreamed that he was guided up a narrow path on the edge of a precipice. Below was a "vast, deep, open, barren space" in which he saw persons "grubbing with their hands in the earth" and "tossing the earth from one hand to the other." They said to one another, "I am countenanced in spending my time in this manner by thee." Shillitoe, sticking close to his guide and realizing the vanity of labor for earthly goods, ascended the path safely. (*Jour.*, 1839, I:51)

John Roberts, when persecuted by a bishop, dreamed that he met a bear in a narrow way. Assured by a shining figure that it was harmless, he got by safely. As a result of this dream he went to the bishop, whom he readily confounded by his sharp wit (*Jour.*, 1887, p. 46).

Rhoda M. Coffin (1826-1909), at the time when the evangelical movement was beginning to sweep through western Quakerism, dreamed of a great storm which was dispelled, after she had prayed for deliverance, by "a man glorious to look upon." This assured her that she ought not to be disturbed by the opposition of conservative Friends to prayer meetings. (*Jour.*, 1910, p. 83)

James Bellangee (1788-1853) dreamed that no more children would be born into the Society of Friends because "we had eaten our bread unthankfully," whereupon bread appeared in the dream, over which he prayed with thankfulness. (*Jour.*, 1854, p. 121)

Margaret Lucas, struggling against accepting the doctrine of election, dreamed that she was damned, but later she felt an assurance of God's mercy. (*Jour.*, 1803, p. 44)

Elizabeth Ashbridge, suffering severely as an indentured servant and contemplating suicide, was cured of this temptation when she dreamed that she saw "a grave woman, holding in her right hand a lamp burning, who said, 'I am sent to tell thee, that, if thou wilt return to the Lord thy God who created thee, he will have mercy on thee, and thy lamp shall not be put out in obscurity.' Her lamp then flamed in an extraordinary manner" (*Jour.*, 1807, p. 15).

In these conflicts, the solution appears in the dream itself in symbolic form.

Since Light is the most common symbol used by Friends to designate the impress of the Divine upon the soul, it is to be expected that light, as if physically perceived, would often appear in dreams and visions. We must in this case say both "dreams" and "visions" because, in dealing with light, the distinction between the semi-waking and the sleeping state is particularly difficult to draw. Joshua Evans was apparently awake when "bringing up my father's flock I saw the glory of the Lord shine round me which seemed to exceed the sun at noon-day." He adds that it "was not an external light." (*Jour.*, 1837, p. 5) Of Edward Stabler it is written that when "he was favored with a knowledge, by internal evidence, of the true and spiritual nature of the Christian religion . . . he could hardly persuade himself that an outward light, above that of the sun, did not shine around him, as he followed his daily vocations." (*Jour.*, 1846, p. 38) John Churchman, while he was trying to judge the validity of an inward call to visit Great Britain, records:

> One day, walking alone, I felt myself so weak and feeble that I stood still and by the reverence that covered my mind I knew that the hand of the Lord was on me and his presence round

about so the earth was silent and all flesh brought into stillness, and light went forth with brightness and shone on Great Britain, Ireland, and Holland, and my mind felt the gentle yet strongly drawing cords of that love which is stronger than death which made me say, Lord! go before and strengthen me and I will follow whithersoever Thou leads.

(Jour., 1779, p. 78)

John Woolman, like Mary Alexander, felt that he was awake when there shone on his bed a light accompanied by a voice. The light, he says, was "at the apparent distance of (about) five feet, about nine inches in diameter, and of a clear and easie brightness, and near the center the most radiant." (Jour., 1922, p. 187) But in some cases the Journalist was sure he was dreaming. Jacob Ritter, finding it hard to forgive his enemies, dreamed that a light led him across a desert, where many reptiles and noxious vermin retreated before it. Finally, with great difficulty he followed the light to the top of a mountain. When he awoke he found that "the Christian spirit in my own breast had entirely overcome that spirit of war and revenge." (Jour., pp. 38-40) Here, as in so many cases, the interpretation not obvious to the reader seems obvious to the dreamer because the dream was accompanied by certain feelings not expressed in imagery. It is apparent that, in the case of light, the veil is thin between the subjective and the objective. Whether the vision is subjective or objective is immaterial to the Quaker, for God can use for His purpose either the inward or the outward light.

Dreams being near the border at which knowledge merges into fantasy, science finds it difficult to deal with them. Prophetic dreams are a type which might seem to some to be well beyond the frontier of present scientific knowledge. Journals contain many examples of prophecies miraculously fulfilled. Among these are a number of prophecies through dreams. Some presage death, as was the case with Mary Neale (1717-1757) who saw in a dream her father "in the agonies of death," or the companion of Rebecca Jones who saw Samuel Emlen just at the time of his death, walking over the water to a ship which took him away. (Jour., 1849, p. 277) Jacob Ritter dreamed that he saw his staff broken and knew at once that it was a premonition of his wife's decease. (Jour., p. 44) Such anticipatory imagery may not be prophecy in the usual sense of the term.

A ship's doctor, given to drink, related a dream to Thomas Chalkley. He dreamed that, while drunken, he was brought before a great black dog as judge who condemned him to prison forever. Chalkley told him that the black dog was death. The dreamer's death did actually occur soon after. (*Jour.*, 1749, p. 25) At another time, while a mile away from Philadelphia he saw "in the vision of life, the hand of the Lord stretched over the city and province with a rod in it." He afterwards finds this to be a premonition of a plague that was to overtake the city. (*Ibid.*, p. 200) Rebecca Jones dreamed that John Reynell was "either gone or near going" and that someone was bringing to her from him a plate of soup. The next day a letter arrived from his executor enclosing a legacy. (*Jour.* 1849, p. 83)

In contrast to these, some dreams, occurring during serious illness, prophesy that death will not occur.

David Ferris (*Jour.*, 1855, p. 26) and Jacob Ritter (*Jour.*, p. 35) both had dreams in which the spirit, seen as if it were out of the body, received heavenly assurance that it would return to earth. Thomas Say (1787-1834), educated in Westtown School, was a famous scientist and one of the founders of the Philadelphia Academy of Natural Science. As a young man, he saw during illness a vision of heaven and three persons whom he recognized, going through the celestial gate. As he attempted to step through the gate with them he stepped into his body. On awakening he found that these same three persons had died during his long trance (*Jour.*, 1796, p. 70)* It would be hard to prove that these deaths had not been mentioned in his presence during this supposed unconscious state. Such visions, occurring during serious illness, may belong in a class separate from those which occur when the mind is in a normal state. That they have some significance is evident from John Woolman's vision in illness in which he saw a mass of human beings with whom he was so mixed that he was no longer a separate person and heard a voice say, "John Woolman is dead." Afterward he became convinced that this

---

* See also, *Thomas Say, Early American Naturalist* by H. B. Weiss, 1931.

meant the death of his own will. (*Jour.*, 1922, p. 308)

Other types of dream prophecies occur in the Journals. Joseph Hoag relates at length several childhood visions prophetic of a bitter controversy between two parties in his meeting—one side led by his father and the other by his uncles. (*Jour.*, 1861, pp. 14-15) His most famous vision, experienced in 1803, truthfully predicted divisions not only among Friends but also in other religious bodies. The Civil War and the abolition of slavery were also foreseen. The prediction in the same vision that afterward a "Monarchial Power" would arise in the United States has not as yet been fulfilled. (*Jour.*, p. 378) John Banks (1634-1710), suffering from a paralyzed arm, dreamed as follows:

> I was with dear George Fox: and I thought I said unto him, George, my faith is such that if thou see'st it thy way to lay thy hand upon my shoulder, my arm and hand shall be whole throughout, which remained with me after I awaked two days and nights (that the thing was a true vision).
>
> (*Jour.*, 1712, p. 66)

As a result, John Banks sought out George Fox, told him his vision, and was healed.

Another type of prophetic dream is the vision of a landscape which, according to the dreamer, is found at a later time to exist, down to the least detail, in the world of reality. J. J. Neave (1836-1909) had a vision of

> our dear Saviour with a company of His saints on a hill with a large stretch of woods or bush lying between us, such as I had never then seen. An earnest and intense longing possessed me to go to him but I was shown a cart track going down into this bush, with an intimation that I must follow that, and my desire would in time be granted.
>
> (*Jour.*, 1910, p. 10)

Twenty years later he traveled to Australia and thought he saw the very scene of his vision. The strange trees turned out to be eucalypti. Another example of this sort is recorded by Benjamin Ferris in *Original Settlements on the Delaware* (pp. 251-254). According to this story, Elizabeth Shipley (1690-1777) and her husband, William Shipley, were comfortably and pros-

perously settled on the banks of Ridley Creek near Philadelphia. There, about 1729, Elizabeth had a vision of a beautiful
landscape. Her dream-guide told her that she and her husband
would eventually settle there. Several years later, on a religious
visit, she halted her horse on a hill overlooking the Brandywine
near what is now Wilmington. There, before her, lay the land
of her vision complete in every respect, even to the accompany-
ing sound of an axe. Returning home, she finally succeeded
in persuading her cautious husband to move to this place.
Here, "with his faith in water power and her faith in power
Divine," as Charles Reade puts it in his novel *The Wandering
Heir* (New York: G. Munro, 1878) they became the leading
citizens of the new town of Wilmington. She was a distinguished
minister, visiting England and many parts of America in her
extensive religious labors.

John Churchman, on a visit to London Yearly Meeting in
1753, was concerned over the fact that some Friends, who he
thought were in the right, stated their views so warmly that
they stirred up needless opposition. He dreamed that he saw
two armies, one fully armed and the other unarmed. The unarmed forces were commanded to march forward without defending themselves. This they succeeded in doing successfully
until one of the unarmed soldiers, being hard-pressed, put forth
his hand at arm's length and a sword took off his finger. By
this dream, John Churchman was assured that the Truth is
best defended by those who are so completely selfless that in
defending Truth they are not at the same time defending themselves (*Jour.,* 1779, p. 132).

The Journals of George Fox and John Woolman contain a
number of dreams which, as has already been noted, were omitted by early editors.

This dream is recorded for 1671, when George Fox was
forty-seven years old:

> And I had a vision about the time that I was in this travail
> and sufferings, that I was walking in the fields and many Friends
> were with me, and I bid them dig in the earth, and they did and
> I went down. And there was a mighty vault top-full of people
> kept under the earth, rocks, and stones. So I bid them break open
> the earth and let all the people out, and they did and all the

people came forth to liberty; and it was a mighty place. And when they had done I went on and bid them dig again. They did, and there was a mighty vault full of people, and I bid them throw it down and let all the people out, and so they did.

And I went on again and bid them dig again, and Friends said unto me, 'George, thou finds out all things,' and so there they digged, and I went down, and went along the vault; and there sat a woman in white looking at time how it passed away. And there followed me a woman down in the vault, in which vault was the treasure; and so she laid her hand on the treasure on my left hand and then time whisked on apace; but I clapped my hand upon her and said 'Touch not the treasure.' And then time passed not so swift.

(Jour., 1952 ed., p. 578)

Whether or not the woman who was forbidden to touch the treasure bears any relation to Margaret Fell whom Fox had married two years before—if so, this throws an interesting sidelight on his marriage—it is, of course, impossible to judge.

John Woolman at the age of nine had a dream so vivid that he recorded it in detail in his Journal many years afterward. In this dream the moon ran quickly westward and from it a cloud descended. This cloud, having become a beautiful green tree, withered in the beams of the rising sun. "Then there appeared a being, small of size, moving swift from the north southward, called a Sun Worm." (<i>Jour.</i>, 1922, p. 152) This dream he says was "instructive," but he gives no interpretation of it.

Another dream, which indicates the effect of slavery on Woolman, is related at the conclusion of his Journal but not as part of it. He dreamed that some hunters had brought in a creature which was part fox and part cat. In order to get food to feed this animal, an old negro was hanged. "One woman spoke lightly of it, and signified she was setting at the Tea Table when they hanged him up, and though neither she nor any present said anything against their proceedings, yet she said at the Sight of the Old Man a dying, she could not go on with Tea Drinking" (<i>Ibid.</i>, p. 116). When the dreamer lamented bitterly at this sight, some smiled and said that the negro's flesh was also needed to feed the hounds.

It is probable that these Quaker dreams are not by and large different from other dreams. For the psychologist it may be of interest to note that the dreams and the self-interpretations are wholly typical in content (both in language and meaning) of the personalities of the dreamers. They are spontaneous expressions in the dream state of fundamental spiritual attitudes developed in the waking state. And finally the dreamer utilizes them, as he does his waking depth experiences in meetings or in solitude, as spiritually meaningful insights, comforts, and stimulations. A few characteristic elements will illustrate: The frequent presence of light, whether appearing as near at hand or as coming from a heavenly body, is a characteristic which has already been noted. Another peculiarity is the frequent appearance of a guide. Quakers have continually emphasized obedience to the Inward Guide and it is not surprising that such guidance should appear in dreams. The guide points out the path and offers an explanation of sights on the way. This guide is never deceptive but always possessed of a heavenly quality.

Another frequent characteristic is the sense of religious awe and dread. Rudolph Otto in his *Idea of the Holy* calls this a "numinous quality," an awareness of the daunting presence of a mysterious power before which man is but "dust and ashes." When a Quaker Journalist writes, "my mind was covered with an awfulness," he speaks of a feeling wholly incomprehensible to one who has never felt it. Some of the dreams recorded in the Journals possess an eerie, other-worldly quality, as if the veil of flesh had grown transparent and the world of spirit had shone through, conveying a meaning not with words but with visual signs. The feelings which accompany such an experience are described by Joseph Hoag:

> In the year 1803, probably in the eighth or ninth month, I was one day alone in the fields, and observed that the sun shone clear, but that a mist eclipsed the brightness of its shining.
>
> As I reflected upon the singularity of the event, my mind was struck into a silence, the most solemn I ever remember to have witnessed, for it seemed as if all my faculties were laid low, and unusually brought into deep silence. I said to myself, "What can all this mean? I do not recollect ever before to have been sensible

of such feelings." And I heard a voice from heaven say, "This thou seest, which dims the brightness of the sun, is a sign of the present and coming times."

(*Jour.*, 1861, p. 378)

A sense of dread solemnity was felt to be a sign that the dream or vision was from God. This was the same sign which certified to the divine origin of any other inward experience.

Members of the Society of Friends have been accused of being idealistic dreamers, standing for an impracticable world-order and trusting to an inward guidance based on intuition rather than on reason and the evidence of science. On the other hand, they have quite as often been accused of being too practical and successful in the affairs of this world for their own religious good. These two contradictory comments indicate an extraordinary characteristic of the Quaker faith which at its best has maintained a balance between inward vision and outward evidence. Quakerism is a religion of inwardness, but this inwardness, the Quakers believe, should never be wholly detached from outward checks, based on a divinely illuminated conscious reason, both in oneself and in others. This doctrine, which has often saved Quakerism from superstition and fanaticism, has also saved it from placing too much or too little faith in dreams. Something important is sometimes revealed there, but man must tread warily in these dim and misty regions and not wander too far from the light of the sun.

CHAPTER XIII

*The Religious Philosophy of Friends**

THE CHRISTIAN religion from its beginning has been seriously handicapped by uncertainty regarding its fundamental doctrines. Its Bible, the primary source of its beliefs, is a medley of many different doctrines. The Old Testament and New Testament are the holy books of two quite different religions and each of the two Testaments contains a variety of frequently conflicting statements. The religion of the priests in the Old Testament is quite different from that of the prophets. The priestly religion is based on ritual, while the prophetic is ethical. In the New Testament there are at least eight different interpretations of Christianity, according to Ernest F. Scott's *The Varieties of New Testament Religion* (New York: Scribners, 1923). Two of these interpretations which are the farthest apart from each other are the mysticism of John's Gospel and the ritualistic and priestly religion of the Epistle to the Hebrews. To John, Christ is the Way, the Truth and the Life and is organically related to his followers, as the branch is related to the vine. He is accordingly directly accessible to his followers. In Hebrews, Christ is far off in heaven, sitting on the right hand of God. He is the High Priest who makes intercession with God for the forgiveness of sinners by sacrificing his blood. This doctrine comes directly from Levit-

---

* The Quaker philosophy of religion is dealt with in greater detail in four Pendle Hill pamphlets: #156, *Ethical Mysticism in the Society of Friends;* #161, *The Religion of George Fox;* #173, *Evolution and the Inward Light;* #179, *Light and Life in the Fourth Gospel.*

icus (chapter 16) in which the high priest is described as entering into the Holy of Holies once a year on the Day of Atonement (Yom Kippur), and performing the prescribed rituals. In Leviticus the high priest offers as atonement the blood of bullock and goat while in Hebrews Christ offers his own blood as atonement. The writer of Hebrews considers this ritualistic act in Leviticus as a symbol which foreshadows events in heaven.

No one knows who wrote the Epistle to the Hebrews. Certainly not Paul. It was admitted to the New Testament canon very reluctantly but no book in the New Testament has more influence. Today it forms the basis of the fundamentalism which now represents the most active part of the Christian church. The Epistle to the Hebrews was, also, largely responsible for Christianity becoming a priestly religion like that of Roman Catholicism. In Protestantism priests are not required to secure access to God, the Bible is considered to be the only means to convey divine truth to the believer. Thus in Protestantism man does not have direct access to divine truth except for book or creed, the rituals, and communion. The process of salvation is almost as external to the human soul as in Catholicism. We, accordingly, find in the New Testament two quite different religions, one in John's gospel in which no priest or pastor is needed to secure accession to God and divine truth, and the other in the Letter to the Hebrews in which a priest or book is needed.

At the beginning of the Society of Friends in the middle of the 17th century the religion of the Puritans was largely based on the Letter to the Hebrews with some additions such as predestination and apocalyptic expectations, while the religion of the Quakers was based largely on John's gospel. The writings of George Fox, Robert Barclay, and William Penn, the three principal founders of the Society of Friends, say little regarding salvation through the blood atonement and the need of intercession between man and God. As a result of this difference of opinion the Quakers were ferociously persecuted by the Puritans and were not considered to be Christians at all. Yet the Quakers believed that their religion was based on the New Testament, while they thought that the Puritan's religion was largely based on the Old Testament. Many thousand anti-Quaker books were catalogued by Joseph Smith (*Biblioteca Anti-Quakeriana*, London, 1873). It would be difficult to exceed the virulent tone of the titles of these books. One of the milder is *The History of the Quakers, or All Hell Broke Loose*. Another is *Some Few of the Quakers many Horrid Blasphemies, Heresies, and their Bloody Treasonable Principles, Destructive to Government*. Each book was replied to and the reply was replied to. For example: *The Snake in the Grass; or Satan transformed into an Angel of Light* was answered by *An Antidote against the Venome of the Snake in the Grass*, followed by *Anguis Flagellatus: or a Switch for the Snake*. This series of attacks and replies extended to six volumes. Anyone who believes that Quakerism is a form of Protestantism should read those titles.

Since the Quakers recognized no authority except the Inward Light they were regarded as anarchists. The four Quakers who were hanged in Boston had an easier time than the many who suffered in filthy English dungeons, where more than four hundred lost their lives. The Quaker resistance to Puritan persecution was entirely non-violent and was the most extensive example of non-violent resistance in history; the most extensive in the time it lasted, in the number concerned, and in the sufferings endured.

The Quaker "heresies" include Universalism, Deism, and Mysticism. Universalism holds that men of all religions can be saved if they follow whatever light they have. Deism holds that there is one God but that we are not entirely dependent upon the holy scriptures to discover what he says to men. This means that we can find proof of God's existence by reason as well as by revelation. Mysticism holds that we can know God directly and immediately, and that we can receive his revelations inwardly.

George Fox writes in his Journal:

> . . . they were discoursing of the blood of Christ; and as they were discoursing of it, I saw, through the immediate opening of the invisible Spirit, the blood of Christ. And I cried out among them, and said, "Do ye not see the blood of Christ? see it in your hearts, to sprinkle your hearts and consciences from dead works to serve

the living God." For I saw it, the blood of the New Covenant, how it came into the heart. This startled the professors, who would have the blood only without them and not in them.

(*Jour.*, 1952 ed., p. 23)

Writing to Friends in Carolina, Fox admonished them to appeal to the light in the heathen:

> And if you had sometimes some meetings with the Indian kings and their people, to preach the Gospel of Peace, of Life, and of Salvation to them; for the Gospel is to be preached to every creature; and Christ hath tasted death for every man and died for their sins, that they might come out of death and sin and live to Christ, that died for them, who hath enlightened them with the light which is the Life in himself; and God pours out of this spirit upon all flesh; that is upon all men and women.

(Epistle 371, *Epistles*, 1698)

William Penn speaks of "the principle of God in man, the precious pearl and leaven of the Kingdom, as the only blessed means appointed of God to quicken, convince and sanctify men." (*The Rise and Progress of the People Called Quakers.* Philadelphia: 1870, pp. 19-20)

John Woolman's Journal was criticised by 19th century Orthodox Friends because he did not mention the Trinity or salvation by the blood of Christ. Woolman used, for the Light within, "that which is pure," meaning that which is not contaminated by any fleshly evil, as the means by which we are "saved."

In addition, Quakers did not accept the Trinitarian theology of the Puritans. The Quakers considered the temporal Jesus of Nazareth to be the true incarnation of the eternal Christ, the Creator, and the Light of the world. Martha Routh, speaking of a meeting in Boston attended by the prominent officials of the state, said:

> . . . it was an open time of labour, though in close expostulation, tending to advance the pure principle of Truth above every shadowy performance, name, or profession of religion as the only means of salvation to man.

(*Jour.*, 1796, p. 234)

And Robert Barclay, the only Quaker to write a systematic theology, says:

> By this seed, grace, and word of God, and light wherewith we say every one is enlightened, and hath a measure of it, which strives with him in order to save him, and which may, by the stubbornness and wickedness of man's will, be quenched, bruised, wounded, pressed down, slain and crucified, we understand not the proper essence and nature of God, precisely taken, which is not divisible into parts and measures, as being a most pure, simple being, void of all composition or division, and therefore can neither be resisted, hurt, wounded, crucified, or slain by all the efforts and strength of men; but we understand a spiritual, heavenly and invisible principle, in which God, as Father, Son, and Spirit, dwells; a measure of which divine and glorious life is in all men as a seed, which of its own nature draws, invites, and inclines to God.
>
> (Proposition VI, Section 13)

These words are obviously not Trinitarian, whatever else they may be.

The Quakers also differed from the Puritans and the Anglicans in their belief in the possibility of perfection. This did not mean that they had attained the goal, but rather that they could attain sufficient measure of the Inward Light, however small, by living up to whatever measure of light they had. If they lived up to what they called their "measure," they would not, like the Puritans, feel a sense of continual guilt.

In the Journal of John Roberts (d. 1683) his son Daniel tells the story of a local aristocrat who, being ill, wished to entertain herself by listening to a debate between a Quaker and an Anglican priest. The argument was about perfection in this life and the possibility of salvation.

> Lady: If you would soberly ask and answer each other a few questions, it would divert me, so that I should be less sensible of the pains I lie under.
>
> Priest: It will not edify your ladyship; for I have discoursed with John, and several others of his persuasion, divers times, and I have read their books, and all to no purpose; for they spring from the Papists, and hold the same doctrine the Papists do. *Let John deny it if he can.*
>
> J. R.: I find thou art setting us out in very black character; with

design to affright me; but therein thou wilt be mistaken. I advise thee to say no worse of us than thou canst make out, and then make us so black as thou canst. And if thou canst prove me a Papist in one thing, with the help of God I'll prove thee like them in ten. And this woman who lies here in bed, shall be judge.

Priest: The Quakers hold that damnable doctrine, and dangerous tenet, *of perfection in this life;* and so do the Papists. If you go about to deny it, John, I can prove you hold it.

J. R.:   I would ask thee one question: Dost thou own a purgatory?

Priest: No.

J. R.   Then the Papists, in this case, are wiser than thou. They own the saying of Christ, who told the unbelieving Jews, if they died in their sins, whither he went they could not come. But by thy discourse, thou and thy followers must needs go headlong to destruction; since thou neither ownest a place of purgation after death, nor such a preparation for heaven to be possible in this life, as is absolutely necessary . . . Pray tell this poor woman, whom thou hast been preaching to for thy belly, whether ever or never, she must expect to be freed of her sins, and made fit for the kingdom of heaven; . . .

Priest: No, John, you mistake me: I believe that God Almighty is able of his great mercy to forgive persons their sins, and fit them for heaven, a little before they depart this life.

J. R.:   I believe the same. But if thou wilt limit the Holy One of Israel, how long wilt thou give the Lord to fit a person for his glorious kingdom?

Priest: It may be an hour or two.

J. R.:   My faith is a day or two, as well as an hour or two.

Priest: I believe so too.

J. R.:   Or a week or two.

And my father carried it to a month or two; and so gradually till he brought it to seven years, the priest confessing he believed the same. On which my father thus proceeded:

J. R.:   How could'st thou accuse me of Popery, in holding this doctrine, which thou thyself hast confessed?

At this the priest appeared uneasy, and said to the lady, "Madam, I must beg your excuse; for there's to be a lecture this afternoon, and I must be there." She pressed him to stay to dinner; but he earnestly desired to be excused. So a slice or two being cut off the spit, he ate, and took his leave.

(Jour., 1852, pp. 28-33)

During the course of the 18th century, the Methodist revival exercised an enormous influence on all Christian sects, including the Quakers. This revival persuaded some Quakers to adopt a theology closer to that of the Puritans than to that of the founders of Quakerism.

One reason for this theological muddle was that the Quakers had no written creed and so they lost sight of the doctrines of the founders. The founders had believed that the spirit of truth would reveal further truth as time went on. Here they followed the instructions of Jesus to his disciples: "When the Spirit of truth comes, he will guide you into all the truth." (John XVI:13) But some of those who imitated the Methodists desired a creed to be written. Others, fortunately, remembered the early belief that Friends should follow the leading of the spirit and not a fixed creed. The New Testament could not serve as a creed because there are several different doctrines in it.

As a result of the Methodist revival, many Quaker leaders came to place more emphasis on a literal interpretation of the scriptures, especially the Epistle to the Hebrews, more emphasis on the blood atonement, more emphasis on the historical Christ, and less emphasis on John's gospel and the eternal Christ. Puritan orthodoxy was revived by such Quaker leaders as Stephen Grellet, Joseph Hoag, and Thomas Shillitoe. Others, such as Job Scott, Elias Hicks, John Comly, and John Wilbur made a strong effort to retain the original liberal theology. But the Hicksites did not follow the early Friends in declaring that Jesus Christ was an incarnation of God. Hicks's followers tended to make Christ just another prophet, while Christ to the early Friends was a figure inspiring worship and reverence. Accordingly, although Hicksites were closer to the early Friends in some respects in their theology and, like them, repudiated the doctrine of the blood atonement, they were more rational and intellectual. Hicksite religion was based on the head and not on the heart. It lacked the emotional power and force of early Quakerism that enabled the first Friends to withstand persecution with enthusiasm.

Out of this theological confusion, there emerged four groups: the Orthodox, the Hicksites, the Wilburites, and the Gurneyites. It is difficult to use the words "liberal" and "conservative" in describing these groups since the original Quakers were very liberal compared to the Puritans. If the word conservative is used to mean going back to original principles, it should be applied to modern liberal Quakers. Followers of Joseph John Gurney are "conservative" in the sense that their theology is closest to that of the Puritans but they are not conservative in preserving the beliefs of early Friends.

A quotation from the Journal of Edward Hicks, cousin of Elias Hicks and painter of the *Peaceable Kingdom,* presents a picture of the situation in the Society in 1847:

> The Society of Friends are scattered and divided, and I fear will too soon be subdivided. The two extremes which have produced this, appear to me now to be carrying out their effect. The Orthodox Friends are in two parties called Gurneyites and Wilburites. The Gurneyites are the extreme Orthodox, and are preparing to amalgamate with the Episcopalians as the Episcopalians are preparing to amalgamate with the Roman Catholics. Friends, or what are called Hicksite Friends, are in two parties, which I shall call, for the purpose of explaining my views, Hicksites and Foxites. The Hicksites appear to me fully prepared to unite with the Deists, and finally join the confederacy or conspiracy to destroy the religion of Jesus in its blessed simplicity, and to introduce the reign of reason instead of revelation. The Foxites, or rather the Society of Friends that unite, or are in union with Fox, Penn, and Barclay, with which I include myself, are . . . in a suffering state, . . . which will be most likely to increase. The Friendly Orthodox are in a similar state and condition. Now if the extreme Orthodox or Gurneyites would quietly go to the Episcopalians where they properly belong, and our ultra reformers go to the Unitarians, their right place, and religious Friends and religious Orthodox could hold a conference, and let that "charity that suffereth long and is kind," sit as moderator, I think there would be but little to prevent their uniting again.
>
> *(Memoirs,* 1851, pp. 251-2)

But no charity moderated this division which stunted the growth of the Society and almost wrecked it. There was no Christian love between the groups. Logan Pearsall Smith (1865-1946), in his autobiography, records an experience he had at the age of six or seven:

I remember climbing the wall that surrounded one of the Hicksite meeting-houses, and gazing in on those precincts with all the horror of one who gazes into Hell. Never since have I looked upon any object with such feelings of abomination.

(*Unforgotten Years,* 1938, p. 26)

There was and still is so much confusion regarding the causes of the tragic separation between the Hicksites and Orthodox in 1827-28 that something more should be added about it. Each side had certain assets and liabilities. The Hicksites were aware that their theology was closer to the theology of the founders of Quakerism than the theology of the Orthodox. To show this they published the works of Fox, Penn, and Barclay in 1831. The Hicksites were attacked viciously by the Orthodox for the same reason that the early Quakers were attacked by the Puritans. London Yearly Meeting paid no attention to the letters from the Hicksites regarding their position. Many English Friends had become very wealthy and had married into the Anglican aristocracy. Accordingly the English Quakers became Anglican in their sympathies. Joseph John Gurney was frequently attacked by the Wilburites as being more Anglican than Quaker.

If the principal asset of the Hicksites was the liberal theology of the founders, the principal asset of the Orthodox was a personal devotion to Christ. Devotion to a person, divine or human, is a most powerful force in every religion, whereas the intellectual attachment to a rational belief leads only to empty abstraction. Devotion to the person of Christ was the most potent factor in holding Christians together in the first century. Though the early Christians were divided in their doctrines, the one theology which was possessed by all of them was the belief in the Lordship of Christ. All early Christians accepted Christ as Lord, *Kúpios.* "No one can say 'Jesus is Lord' except by the Holy Spirit." (I Cor. 12:3) A lord is a person, divine or human, who inspires love, affection, and complete obedience. Acceptance of Jesus as Lord was the one test of Orthodoxy in all the eight varieties of New Testament religion mentioned by Scott. That Christ was worshiped as Lord was illustrated by William Penn's experience. Penn wrote a book entitled *Sandy Foundation Shaken* (1668) which contains all the usual Quaker heresies such as Universalism, Deism, and others. As the result Penn was imprisoned in the Tower of London. There he wrote a second book entitled *Innocency with her open Face* (1669). In this book he emphasized so strongly the lordship and divinity of Christ that he was released. His persecutors failed to notice that he never mentioned the holy spirit, since for Penn the holy spirit was the Christ Within. Whittier in his poem "Our Master" testifies to the Lordship of Christ. The poem could be titled "Our Lord" instead of "Our Master."

Thus, although the Orthodox adopted a theology like that of the Puritans who persecuted Quakers, the Hicksites were unable to convince the English Quakers and others that they had what was substantially the theology of the founders of Quakerism. Accordingly, Orthodox Quakerism had more emotional force, while the Hicksites had a religion which was more intellectually acceptable.

Eventually reconciliation between Orthodox and Hicksites began to take place. The "Hicksites" and the "Orthodox"—except for the extreme Gurneyites*—reunited in Philadelphia, New York, New England, and Canada, a gradual process which culminated formally in the 1950's. The groups which united discovered that they supplemented each other. Together they form a more complete religion because this religion includes both head and heart or, in other words, both intellect and feeling. The reunion contains no vestige of the former hostility, although a few differences certainly remain. The result is a stronger Society of Friends than either party itself would constitute.

The Puritan theology has not been consciously repudiated so much as gradually ignored. Partly through higher education, partly through better knowledge of Quaker history, and partly through indifference to all dogmatic theologies, a liberal theology has become more prominent among the groups of Friends who united, a theology closer in many ways to the original

---

* The Gurneyites could not unite because they had accepted a Methodist form of worship. In 1887 a Conference of Friends in Richmond, Indiana, wrote an evangelical creed, called a "Declaration of Faith," which was adopted in 1922 by the Five Years Meeting, made up of Gurneyite Friends.

theology of the founders of Quakerism based on "salvation" through the Inward Light.

But the doctrine of the Atonement, so much a part of orthodox Christianity, has not been completely rejected. When Paul says, "Christ in you, the hope of glory," (Col., 1:27) he expresses clearly the Quaker conception. But Paul also says: "In him we have redemption through his blood." (Eph. 1:7) This confusion may occur within a single verse: "For if while we were enemies we were reconciled to God by the death of his Son, much more, now that we are reconciled, shall we be saved by his life." (Rom. 5:10) Here we have John Wesley and Robert Barclay in the same verse. Quakerism emphasizes religious experience and has little room for that which happened long ago and far away, but the historical origin of the Christian religion must not be ignored.

Josiah Royce, in his work entitled *The Problem of Christianity* (New York: Macmillian, 1913), gives us a theory of the atonement of Christ which comes close to expressing the original Quaker view.

> . . . in this discussion I am speaking of the purely human aspect of the idea of atonement. *That* aspect is now capable of a statement which does not pretend to deal with any but our human world, and which fully admits the pettiness of every human individual effort to produce such a really atoning deed. . . . The human community, depending, as it does, upon its loyal human lovers, and wounded to the heart by its traitors, . . . utters its own doctrine of atonement . . . This postulate I word thus: *No baseness or cruelty of treason so deep or so tragic shall enter our human world, but that loyal love shall be able in due time to oppose to just that deed of treason its fitting deed of atonement.* The deed of atonement shall be so wise and so right in its efficacy, that the spiritual world, after the atoning deed, shall be better, richer, more triumphant amidst all its irrevocable tragedies, than it was before that traitor's deed was done. . . . The Christian symbol and the practical postulates are two sides of the same life,—at once human and divine.
>
> (Vol. I:320-3)

This doctrine of the atonement is based on Royce's theory of the community. The act of atonement as the means by which the unity of the community may be restored is not central in Quaker theology. But the Quaker society was communitarian in structure, and those who destroyed the unity of the community by some disloyal act were required by the Quaker business meeting to restore that unity by making an apology or performing some act of atonement.

The Quaker theory of atonement, based on immediate human experience rather than on something that has happened in history, may be seen in these quotations from the Journal of Stephen Crisp (1628-1692).

> The source of evil in human nature was the evil inclinations of the flesh and accordingly the flesh must be crucified if the spiritual is to be resurrected.
>
> The cross of Christ was laid upon me, and I bore it. As I came willingly to take it up, I found it to be to me, that thing which I had sought from my childhood, even the power of God, for by it I was crucified to the world, and it to me, which nothing else could ever do.
>
> (*Jour.*, F.L. XIV:142-3)

The Greek philosophy of Stoicism, which thought of God as the soul of the universe, had a great influence throughout the Mediterranean world about the time when the New Testament was written. Near the end of the first century an important addition was made to the Stoic philosophy which leaves in it a place for the eternal Christ. From Stoicism the writer of the Gospel of John appropriated the concept of the Logos. According to John, the eternal Christ was the Logos (translated as "Word") of God who existed from the beginning (John 1:1). And in John we find the Logos described as the Creator, the Light, and the Life of man, which was of God and from God. "All things were made through him, and without him was not anything made that was made. In him was life, and the life was the light of men." (John 1:3, 4) The ninth verse of the first chapter of John was quoted by Barclay as the "Quaker verse." This is as follows: "That was the true Light, which lighteth every man that cometh into the world." (King James Version) This was mistranslated in the Revised Standard Version to apply only to a temporal event. John Wilbur (1774-

1856) accused Joseph John Gurney of a similar misapprehension. " 'That was the true light which lighteth every man that cometh into the world,' he (Gurney) construes to mean no more than Christ incarnate" (*Jour.*, 1859, p. 286).

The whole Gospel of John was written to show how this eternal Christ, or Logos, operates in creating and evolving the world. Many quotations from Fox, Penn, and Barclay could be cited to indicate that they were thinking primarily of the eternal Christ, the Logos or "Word" of God as Creator and Savior and that the temporal Christ was not just a symbol of the eternal Christ but actually a personification of him.

If we think of God as a person in the same sense that we are persons, we can observe the duality in God as well as in ourselves. We are not one, but two. One self is known only to ourselves; the other self is known to others. In the same way God the Father and his outward manifestation, God the Son, form the duality of God. We can know God the Father indirectly through the actions and the inward voice, the inward light, of his Son, Christ the Creator.

Christ as the incarnation of God is worthy of reverence and worship. In John's gospel, because the Inward Christ is a light in all men, he could say: "I am the Way, the Truth and the Life." This Christ could pray to his father, "The glory which thou hast given me I have given to them, that they may be one even as we are one, I in them and thou in me, that they may become perfectly one, so that the world may know that thou hast sent me and hast loved them even as thou hast loved me." (John XVII: 22, 23) John Greenleaf Whittier, who can be properly claimed by the liberal wing of the Society of Friends, says in his poem entitled "Our Master":

> No fable old, nor mythic lore,
> > Nor dream of bards and seers,
> No dead fact stranded on the shore
> > Of the oblivious years:—
> But warm, sweet, tender even yet
> > A present help is he;
> And faith has still its Olivet,
> > And love its Galilee.

Obviously Whittier is not speaking here of an ordinary man but of an incarnation of God. If Christ were only a great prophet he would not inspire the holy dread and reverence felt by his followers.

Awe and reverence for Christ, both historic and eternal, are parts of the very existence of Christianity. We see Christ as Francis Thompson did: "And lo, Christ walking on the water not of Gennesareth but Thames" ("The Kingdom of God," *The Complete Poems of Francis Thompson,* New York: Boni and Liveright, 1913, p. 356). This divine Christ's spirit is the heart and soul of every genuine Christian worship. John in his gospel describes the Christ Within as the light which enlightens every man. But this does not make the divine presence commonplace, any more than the historic Christ was commonplace. Events described in the gospels show him to be far from an ordinary person. The Christ spirit is, rather, a divine incarnation of God himself as a present day reality.

In hearing the Son we hear the Father also . . . as God did then speak by his Son in the days of his flesh, so the Son, Christ Jesus, doth now speak by his Spirit. . . . They that come to be renewed up again into the divine, heavenly image, in which man was at first made, will know the same God, that was the first teacher of Adam and Eve in Paradise, to speak to them now by his son who changes not. Glory be to his name for ever!

(George Fox, *Jour.* [1952 ed.], p. 666)

Bibliography

Autobiographical and Biographical Works Cited

Alexander, Mary (1760-1810), *Some Account of the Life and Religious Experience*. Philadelphia: B. and T. Kite, 1815.

Allen, William (1770-1843). *Life of William Allen,* 2 vols. Philadelphia: Longstreth, 1847.

Alsop, Christine Majolier (1805-1879), *Memorials,* compiled by Martha Braithwaite. London: Samuel Harris & Co. 1881.

Arnett, Thomas (1791-1877), *Journal of the Life, Travels, and Gospel Labors.* Chicago: Publishing Association of Friends, 1884.

Ashbridge, Elizabeth (1713-1755), *Some Account of the Life of Elizabeth Ashbridge, written by herself.* Philadelphia: Friends Book Store.

Bangs, Benjamin (1652-1741), *Memoirs of the Life and Convincement.* Friends' Library, v.IV. Philadelphia: 1840.

Banks, John (1634-1710), *A Journal of the Labours, Travels, and Sufferings of the Faithful Minister of Jesus Christ, John Banks,* Friends Library v.II. Philadelphia: 1838.

Barclay, John (1797-1838), *A Selection from the Letters and Papers,* Philadelphia: Friends Book Store, 1877.

Bassett, Hannah (1815-1853), *Memoir of Hannah Bassett, with Extracts from Her Diary.* Lynn, Mass.: W. W. Kellogg, 1860.

Battey, Thomas C. (1826-1897), *The Life and Adventures of a Quaker Among the Indians.* Boston: Lee and Shepard, 1875.

Bean, Joel (1825-1914), "Recollections of Childhood," *Bulletin of the Friends Historical Association* XXXIX (Autumn, 1950), 102.

Bellangee, James (1788-1853), *Journal and Essays on Religious Subjects.* Bordentown, N.J.: Aaron Bellangee, 1854.

Bownas, Samuel (1676-1753), *An Account of the Life, Travels, and Christian Experiences in the Work of the Ministry.* Stanford, N.Y.: Henry Hull, 1805.

Burnyeat, John (1631-1690), *Journal of the Life and Gospel Labours.* Friends' Library, v.XI. Philadelphia: 1847.

Burrough, Edward (1634-1662), *A Memoir of a Faithful Servant of Christ and Minister of the Gospel who Died in Newgate.* London: Charles Gilpin, 1851.

Catchpool, Corder (1883-1952), *On Two Fronts.* London: Headley Bros. 1918.

Caton, William (1636-1665), *Journal of the Life of that Faithful Servant and Minister of the Gospel of Jesus Christ.* Friends' Library, v.IX. Philadelphia: 1845.

Chace, Elizabeth Buffum (1806-1899), *Two Quaker Sisters.* New York: Liveright, 1937. (from the original diaries of Elizabeth Buffum Chace and Lucy Buffum Lovell.)

Chalkley, Thomas (1675-1741), *Journal or Historical Account of the Life, Travels, and Christian Experiences.* Philadelphia: James Chattin, 1754.

Churchman, John (1705-1775), *An Account of the Gospel Labours and Christian Experiences of a Faithful Minister of Christ.* Philadelphia: Joseph Crukshank, 1779.

Clark, Roger (1871-1961), *Quaker Inheritance.* A portrait of Roger Clark of Street based on his own writings and correspondence by Percy Lovell. London: The Bannisdale Press, 1970.

Coffin, Levi (1798-1877) *Reminiscences.* Cincinnati: Robert Clarke & Co., 1880.

Coffin, Rhoda M. (1826-1909), *Reminiscences, Addresses, Papers, and Ancestry.* New York: Grafton, 1910.

Collins, Elizabeth (1755-1831) *Memoirs of Elizabeth Collins.* Philadelphia: Friends Book Store, 1859.

Comly, John (1773-1850), *Journal of the Life and Religious Labours.* Philalelphia: T. Ellwood Chapman, 1853.

Comstock, Elizabeth L. (1815-1891), *Life and Letters,* Compiled by her Sister, C. Hare. Philadelphia: John C. Winston & Co., 1895.

Cope, Edward (1840-1897) *Cope: Master Naturalist.* Princeton: Princeton University Press, 1931.

Cornell, John J. (1826-1909), *Autobigraphy.* Baltimore: Lord Baltimore, 1906.

Coxere, Edward (1633-1694), *Adventures by Sea.* Edited by E. H. W. Meyerstein, with a foreword by H. M. Tomlinson. New York: Oxford University Press, 1946.

Crisp, Stephen (1628-1692), *The Christian Experiences, Gospel Labors, and Writings.* Friends' Library, v.XIV. Philadelphia: 1850.

Crook, John (1627-1699), *Selections from the Writings,* to which is prefixed a short account of his life written by himself. Friends' Library, v.XIII. Philadelphia: 1849.

Dickenson, Jonathan (1663-1704) *God's Protecting Providence, Man's Surest Help and Defence in Times of Greatest Difficulty and Most Imminent Danger.* London: James Phillips, 1787.

Dickinson, James (1659-1741), *A Journal of the Life and Travels,* Friends' Library, v.xii. Philadelphia: 1848.

Drinker, Elizabeth (1734-1807), *Extracts from the Journal, from 1759 to 1807 A.D.,* Edited by Henry D. Biddle. Philadelphia: Lippincott, 1889.

Edmundson, William (1627-1712), *A Journal of the Life, Travels, Sufferings and Labour of Love in the Work of the Ministry.* London: Mary Hinde, 1774.*

Ellwood, Thomas (1639-1713), *The History of the Life of Thomas Ellwood, Or, an Account of his Birth, Education, etc.* London: J. Sowle, 1714.

Evans, Joshua (1731-1798), *A Journal of the Life, Travels, Religious Exercises, and Labours in the Work of the Ministry.* Byberry, Pa.: John and Isaac Comly, 1837.

Evans, William (1787-1867), *Journal of the Life and Religious Services.* Philadelphia: Friends' Book Store, 1870.

Ferris, David (1707-1799), *Memoirs of the Life of David Ferris.* Philadelphia: Merrihew & Thompson, 1855. (Merrihew & Thompson's Steam Power Press).

First Publishers of Truth. Ed. by Norman Penney for Friends Historical Society, London, 1907.

Fothergill, Samuel (1715-1772), *Memoirs of the Life and Gospel Labors.* New York: Baker & Crane, 1844.

Fox, Caroline (1819-1871), *Memories of Old Friends, . . . from the Journals and letters of Caroline Fox of Penferrick, Cornwall, from 1835 to 1871,* edited by Horace N. Pym. Philadelphia: Lippincott, 1882.

Fox, George (1624-1690), *The Journal of George Fox,* A revised edition by John L. Nickalls. Cambridge: Cambridge University Press, 1952.

Fry, Elizabeth (1780-1845), *Memoir of the Life of Elizabeth Fry with extracts from her journal and letters,* Edited by two of her daughters. Philadelphia: J. W. Moore, 1847.

Garrett, Alfred Cope (1867-1946), *One Mystic.* 1946.

Gough, James (1712-1780) *Some Account of the Life and Gospel Labours of William Reckitt, late of Lincolnshire in Great-Britain, also Memoirs of the Life, Religious Experiences, and Gospel Labours of James Gough, late of Dublin deceased.* Philadelphia: Joseph Crukshank, 1783.

---

* The dramatic events in Edmundson's Journal are not cited in the text, since an abbreviated edition of the Journal has been recently published, edited by Caroline Jacob (Philadelphia Yearly Meeting, 1968).

Gratton, John (1643-1711), *A Journal of the Life of that Ancient Servant of Christ.* Stanford, N.Y.: Henry Hull, 1805.

Grellet, Stephen (1773-1855), *Memoirs of the Life and Gospel Labors of Stephen Grellet.* Philadelphia: Friends' Book Store, 2nd American edition, n.d.

Grubb, Sarah (1756-1790), *An Account of the Life and Religious Labours.* London: Phillips, 1794.

Gurney, Joseph John (1788-1847), *Memoirs,* with selections from his journal and correspondence (2 vols.) Philadelphia: Lippincott, Grambo & Co., 1854.

Hagger, Mary (1758-1840), *Extracts from the Memoranda of Mary Hagger, Ashford, Kent.* Friends' Library, v.VII. Philadelphia, 1843.

Hall, David (1683-1758), *Some Brief Memoirs of the Life of David Hall.* Friends Library, v. XIII. Philadelphia, 1849.

Hall, Rufus (1744-1805), *A Journal of the Life, Religious Exercises and Travels in the Work of the Ministry.* Byberry, Pa., John & Isaac Comly, 1840.

Hallowell, Benjamin (1799-1877), *Autobiography.* Philadelphia: Friends' Book Association, 1883.

Henderson, James (1859-1942), *An Autobiography of the Life and Religious Experiences.* Ohio Yearly Meeting, 1944.

Hicks, Edward (1780-1849), *Memoirs of the Life and Religious Labors of Edward Hicks.* Philadelphia: Merrihew & Thompson, 1851.

Hicks, Elias (1748-1830), *Journal of the Life and Religious Labors of Elias Hicks.* New York: Isaac T. Hopper, 1832.

Hoag, Joseph (1762-1853), *Journal.* Auburn, N.Y.: Auburn Journal Office, 1861.

Hobhouse, Stephen (1881-1951), *Autobiography.* Boston: Beacon Press, 1952.

Hopper, Isaac T. (1771-1852), *A True Life,* by L. Maria Child. Cleveland, Ohio: John P. Jewett & Co., 1853.

Howard, Luke (1772-1864), *Love and Truth in Plainness Manifested,* being a collection of the several Writings, Faithful Testimonies, and Christian Epistles, of that Ancient Suffering Servant and Minister of Christ, Luke Howard. London: T. Sowle, 1707.

Howgill, Francis (1618-1668), *Francis Howgill's Testimony Concerning the Life, Death, Tryals, Travels and Labours of Edward Burrough, 1662.* in *Works of Edward Burrough compiled by Ellis Hookes.* London: 1672.

Hubben, William (b.1895), *Exiled Pilgrim.* New York: Macmillan, 1943.

Hunt, Sarah (1797-1889), *Journal of the Life and Religious Labors of Sarah Hunt*. Philadelphia: Friends' Book Association, 1892.

Janney, Samuel M. (1801-1880), *Memoirs*. Philadelphia: Friends' Book Association, 1881.

Jay, Allen (1831-1910), *Autobiography*. Philadelphia: John C. Winston, 1910.

Jones, Rebecca (1739-1818), *Memorials of Rebecca Jones compiled by William J. Allinson*. Philadelphia: Henry Longstreth, 1849.

Jones, Rufus (1863-1948), *Finding the Trail of Life*. New York: Macmillan, 1929.

Jordan, Richard (1756-1826), *A Journal of the Life and Religious Labours*. Philadelphia: Thomas Kite, 1829.

Judge, Hugh (1750-1834), *Memoirs and Journal*. Byberry, Pa.: John and Isaac Comly, 1841.

Kersey, Jesse (1768-1846), *A Narrative of the Early Life, Travels, and Gospel Labors*. Philadelphia: T. Ellwood Chapman, 1851.

Latey, Gilbert (1626-1708), *A Brief Narrative of the Life and Death of that Ancient Servant of the Lord and his People, Gilbert Latey*. London: T. Sowle, 1707.

Logan, Deborah Norris (1761-1839), "Extracts from the Journal of Deborah Logan" compiled by Barbara Hopkins Jones, in the Haverford College Library.

Lucas, Margaret (1701-1769), *An Account of the Convincement and Call to the Ministry*. Stanford, N.Y.: Henry & John Hull, 1803.

Lundy, Benjamin (1789-1839), *The Life, Travels and Opinions of Benjamin Lundy*. Philadelphia: William D. Parrish, 1847.

Marshall, Charles (1637-1698), *The Journal of that Faithful Minister of Christ Jesus*. Friends Library, v.IV. Philadelphia: 1840.

Martin, Isaac (1758-1828), *A Journal of the Life, Travels, Labours, and Religious Exercises*. Philadelphia: William P. Gibbons, 1834.

Mifflin, Warner (1745-1798), *Life and Ancestry of Warner Mifflin compiled by Hilda Justice*. Philadelphia: Ferris & Leach, 1905.

Neale, Mary (1717-1757), *Some Account of the Religious Experiences of Mary Neale, formerly Mary Peisley, principally compiled from her own writings*. Dublin: John Gough, 1795.

Neave, J. J. (1836-1909), *Leaves from the Journal of Joseph James Neave*. London: Headly Bros. 1910.

Newport, Elizabeth (1796-1872), *Memoir compiled by Ann A. Townsend*. Philadelphia: Friends' Book Association, 1878 (2d ed.).

Nitobe, Inazo (1862-1933), *Reminiscences of Childhood*. Tokyo: Maruzen Co., 1934.

Pearson, Anthony (1628-1707), *Letters, &c of Early Friends*. Letter No. 3, Anthony Pearson to George Fox, London, 30th of 5th mo. (7th mo.) 1654. London: Harvey and Darton, 1841.

Pemberton, Israel (1715-1779), *Israel Pemberton, King of the Quakers*, by Theodore Thayer. Philadelphia: Historical Society of Pennsylvania, 1943.

Penington, Mary (1625-1682), *Experiences in the Life of Mary Penington*. Philadelphia: The Biddle Press, c.1910.

Penn, William (1644-1718), "Author's Travels in Holland and Germany," *Select Works of William Penn, to which is prefixed a Journal of His Life*. London: 1771.

Phillips, Catherine (1726-1794), *Memoirs of the Life of Catherine Phillips*. Philadelphia: Robert Johnson & Co., 1798.

Pike, Joseph (1657-1729), *Some Account of the Life of Joseph Pike*. Friends' Library, v.II. Philadelphia: 1838.

Price, Philip (1764-1837)

Price, Rachel (d.1847), *Memoir of Philip and Rachel Price*. Printed for Eli K. Price and Philip M. Price. Philadelphia: 1852.

Pringle, Cyrus (1838-1911), *The Civil War Diary of Cyrus Pringle*. Wallingford, Pa.: Pendle Hill Pamphlet #122, 1962.

Reade, Charles (1814-1884), *The Wandering Heir*. New York: G. Munro, 1878.

Richardson, George (1773-1863), *Journal of the Gospel Labours of George Richardson, a Minister in the Society of Friends, with a Biographical Sketch of his Life and Character*. London: Alfred Bennett, 1864.

Richardson, John (1666-1753), *An Account of that Ancient Servant of Jesus Christ*. Philadelphia: Friends' Book Store, 1856.

Ritter, Jacob (1756-1841), *Memoirs,* Ed. Joseph Foulke. Philadelphia: T. E. Chapman, 1844.

Roberts, John (d.1683), *Some Memoirs of the Life of John Roberts written by his son, Daniel Roberts*. Philadelphia: Henry Longstreth, 1852.

Routh, Martha (1743-1817), *Memoir of the Life, Travels, and Religious Experience*. York: W. Alexander & Son, 1822.

Russell, Elbert (1871-1951), *Elbert Russell, Quaker. An Autobiography*. Jackson, Tenn.: Friendly Press, 1956.

Rutty, John (1698-1775), *A Spiritual Diary and Soliloquies*. London: James Phillips, 1796.

Sargent, John G. (1813-1883), *Selections from the Diary and Correspondence*. Newport, Mon., 1885.

Savery, William (1750-1804), *A Journal of the Life, Travels, and Religious Labors, compiled from his original memoranda by Jonathan Evans*. Philadelphia: Friends' Book Store, 1863.

Say, Thomas (1709-1796), *A Short compilation of the Life of Thomas Say*. Philadelphia: Budd and Bartram, 1796.

Scattergood, Thomas (1748-1814), *Journal of the Life and religious labors of Thomas Scattergood, a Minister of the Gospel, in the Society of Friends*. Stereotype edition. Philadelphia: n.d.

Scott, Job (1751-1793), *Journal of the Life, Travels, and Religious Labours, and Christian Experiences of that Faithful Servant and Minister of Christ, to which are added Remarks on the Nature of Salvation by Christ*. Philadelphia: John Comly, 1831.

Sharpless, Isaac (1848-1920), *The Quaker Boy on the Farm and at School*. Philadelphia: The Biddle Press; London: Headley Bros., 1908.

Shillitoe, Thomas (1754-1836), *Journal of the Life, Labours, and Travels* (2 vols.) London: Harvey and Darton, 1839 (2d ed.).

Smith, John (1722-1771), *Hannah Logan's Courtship, A True Narrative. The Wooing of the daughter of James Logan, Colonial Governor of Pennsylvania . . . as related in the diary of her lover, the Honorable John Smith, Esq. Edited by Albert Cook Myers*. Philadelphia: Ferris and Leach, 1904.

Smith, Logan Pearsall (1865-1946), *Unforgotten Years*. London: Constable & Co., Ltd., 1938.

Stabler, Edward (1769-1831), *A Memoir of the Life of Edward Stabler, with a collection of his letters, by his son, William Stabler*. Philadelphia. Byberry, Pa.: John Comly, 1846.

Stephen, Caroline Emelia (1834-1909), *Quaker Strongholds*. London: Kegan Paul, Trench, Trubner & Co., Ltd., 1890.

Stephenson, Sarah (1738-1831), *Memoirs of the Life and Travels*. Philadelphia: Kimber, Conrad & Co., 1807.

Stirredge, Elizabeth (1634-1706), *Strength in Weakness Manifest in the Life, Various Trials, and Christian Testimony of that Faithful Servant and Handmaid of the Lord, Elizabeth Stirredge*. Philadelphia: Benjamin & Thomas Kite, 1810.

Story, Christopher (1648-1720), *A Brief Account of the Life, Convincement, Sufferings, Labours and Travels of that Faithful Elder and Minister of Christ Jesus, Christopher Story*. London: J. Sowle, 1726.

Story, Thomas (1666-1720), *A Journal of the Life of Thomas Story*. Newcastle upon Tyne: Isaac Thompson & Co., 1747.

Taylor, George (1803-1891), *Autobiography and Writings*. Philadelphia: 1891. (George Taylor was connected for many years with *The Friend* and *The Friends' Review*. His journal was presumably published by friends in the publishing business.)

Taylor, Hannah (1774-1812), *Memoir of Hannah Taylor, extracted from her own memorandums*. York: W. Alexander, 1820. (Bound with the Memoir of Martha Routh).

Tuke, Samuel (1784-1851), *Samuel Tuke, His Life, Work, and Thoughts compiled by Charles Tyler*. London: Headley Brothers, 1900.

Warder, Ann Head (1758-1829), "Diary," 14 vols. in MS presented in 1923 to Historical Society of Pennsylvania.

Wheeler, Daniel (1771-1840), *Diary of Daniel Wheeler while engaged in a religious visit to the islands of the South Pacific, accompanied by his son, Charles Wheeler*. Philadelphia: 1840.

_____, *Memoirs of the Life and Gospel Labors*. Philadelphia: Friends' Book Store, 1859 (Reprinted from the London Edition).

White, Barclay, (1821-1906), "Journal 1821-1903" MS, in family residence, 120 Hilldale Road, Lansdowne, Pa.

Whitehead, George (1636-1722), *The Christian Progress of That Ancient Servant and Minister of Jesus Christ, George Whitehead . . .* In four parts. London: J. Sowle, 1725.

Whitehead, John (1630-1696), *The Enmity Between the Two Seeds . . . Also a Declaration of the ground and manner of my imprisonment . . . 1655*. (See Smith, Joseph, *A Descriptive Catalogue of Friends' Books*. London: 1867, II, 909-910.)

Wilbur, John (1774-1856), *Journal of the Life of John Wilbur*. Providence: George H. Whitney, 1859. .

Wister, Sally (1761-1804), *Sally Wister's Journal*, ed. Albert Cook Myers. Philadelphia: Ferris and Leach, 1902.

Woolman, John (1720-1772), *The Journal and Essays, edited from the original manuscripts with a biographical introduction by Amelia Mott Gummere*. Philadelphia: Friends Book Store, 1922.

Yeardley, John (1786-1858), *Memoir and Diary, edited by Charles Tylor*. Philadelphia: Longstreth, 1860.

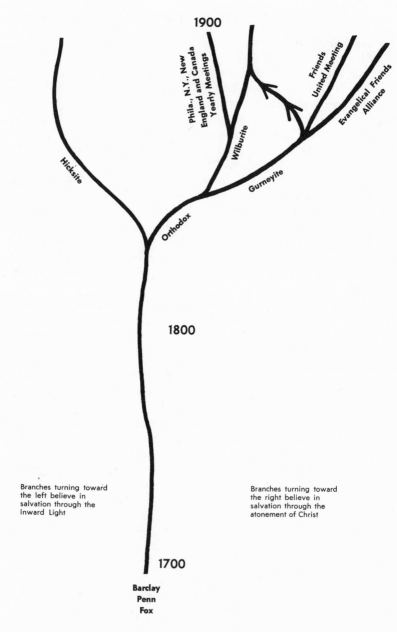

1900

Phila., N.Y., New England and Canada Yearly Meetings

Friends United Meeting

Evangelical Friends Alliance

Wilburite

Hicksite

Gurneyite

Orthodox

1800

Branches turning toward the left believe in salvation through the Inward Light

Branches turning toward the right believe in salvation through the atonement of Christ

1700

Barclay
Penn
Fox

DIVISIONS IN AMERICAN QUAKERISM BASED ON THEOLOGY